THE
ABSENT
CHRIST

The C. Henry Smith series is edited by J. Denny Weaver. Volumes to date have been released by Cascadia Publishing House (originally Pandora Press U.S., a name some of the earlier series books carry) and frequently copublished by Herald Press in cooperation with Bluffton University as well as the Mennonite Historical Society. Bluffton University, in consultation with the publishers, is primarily responsible for the content of the studies.

1. Anabaptists and Postmodernity
   Edited by Susan Biesecker-Mast and Gerald Biesecker-Mast, 2000

2. Anabaptist Theology in Face of Postmodernity:
   A Proposal for the Third Millennium
   By J. Denny Weaver, 2000

3. Fractured Dance:
   Gadamer and a Mennonite Conflict over Homosexuality:
   By Michael A. King, 2001

4. Fixing Tradition: Joseph W. Yoder, Amish American
   By Julia Kasdorf, 2002

5. Walker in the Fog: On Mennonite Writing
   By Jeff Gundy, 2005

6. Separation and the Sword in Anabaptist Persuasion:
   Radical Confessional Rhetoric from Schleitheim to Dordrecht
   By Gerald Biesecker-Mast, 2006

7. Searching for Sacred Ground:
   The Journey of Chief Lawrence Hart, Mennonite
   By Raylene Hinz-Penner, 2007

8. Practicing the Politics of Jesus:
   The Origin and Significance of John Howard Yoder's Social Ethics
   By Earl Zimmerman, 2007

9. Peace to War:
   Shifting Allegiances in the Assemblies of God
   By Paul Alexander, 2009

10. Songs from an Empty Cage:
    Poetry, Mystery, Anabaptism, and Peace
    By Jeff Gundy, 2013

11. Education with the Grain of the Universe:
    A Peaceable Vision for the Future of Mennonite Schools,
    Colleges, and Universities
    Edited by J. Denny Weaver, 2017

12. The Absent Christ:
    An Anabaptist Theology of the Empty Tomb
    Justin Heinzekehr, 2019

THE
ABSENT
CHRIST

An Anabaptist
Theology of the
Empty Tomb

Justin Heinzekehr

The C. Henry Smith Series
Volume 12

Cascadia
Publishing House
Telford, Pennsylvania

Cascadia Publishing House orders, information, reprint permissions:
contact@CascadiaPublishingHouse.com
1-215-723-9125
126 Klingerman Road, Telford PA 18969
www.CascadiaPublishingHouse.com

The Absent Christ
Copyright © 2019 by Cascadia Publishing House,
a division of Cascadia Publishing House LLC
Telford, PA 18969
All rights reserved.
ISBN 13: 13: 978-1-68027-014-3 **ISBN 10:** 1-68027-014-1
Book design by Cascadia Publishing House
Cover design by Dawn Ranck Hower

Library of Congress Cataloguing-in-Publication Data
Copy coming
Names: Heinzekehr, Justin, author.
Title: The absent Christ : an Anabaptist theology of the empty tomb / Justin Heinzekehr.
Description: Telford, Pennsylvania : Cascadia Publishing House, 2019. |
  Series: The C. Henry Smith series ; Volume 12 | Includes bibliographical references.
Identifiers: LCCN 2019002154| ISBN 9781680270143 (trade pbk. : alk. paper) |
  ISBN 1680270141 (trade pbk. : alk. paper)
Subjects: LCSH: Jesus Christ--Resurrection. | Anabaptists--Doctrines.
Classification: LCC BT482 .H45 2019 | DDC 232/.5--dc23
LC record available at https://lccn.loc.gov/2019002154

25 24 23 22 21 20 19   10 9 8 7 6 5 4 3 2 1

To
Hannah, Ellie, and Conrad

CONTENTS

Series Editor's Preface   *11*
Author's Preface   *13*
Introduction: The Voice of the Most High   *17*

Chapter One: The Cords of the Grave: The Primacy of the Empty
    Tomb • *31*

Chapter Two: Foundations Laid Bare: Radical Re-formation • *45*

Chapter Three: Spacious Place: Theology through the Tomb • *58*

Chapter Four: Un/godly Floods: Metaphysics after the Tomb • *70*

Chapter Five: The King and the Enemy: Traces of Sovereignty • *84*

Chapter Six: The Reeling Earth:
    Eco-Theology in the Absence of Christ • *96*

Chapter Seven: The Cleanness of My Hands:
    Topographical Pacifism • *107*

Conclusion   *120*
Notes   *128*
Bibliography   *146*
The Index   *153*
The Author   *159*

SERIES EDITOR'S PREFACE

Justin Heinzekehr's *The Absent Christ: An Anabaptist Theology of the Empty Tomb*, is an important work of creative theologizing. Its significance comes from the fact that it assumes a contemporary worldview, and uses the language and imagery of that worldview to talk about the meaning of Jesus. The practice of making such contemporary restatements stands in a long tradition, which began already in the New Testament.

Six sermonic narratives by the apostles in Acts identify Jesus by recounting his story, some a quite lengthy recitation, others a bare outline (Acts 2:14-36; 3:12-26; 4:8-12; 5:29-32; 10:34-43; 13:16-41). New Testament writers then took that narrative into other contexts or worldviews, and used the language of that new context to express the meaning of Jesus as identified both with the realm of God and the arena of human beings. The result was depictions of Jesus in terms of the Word who became flesh in John 1, as Creator and first fruits of creation in Colossians 1, as High Priest in Hebrews, as New Adam in Philippians 2, and as slain and resurrected Lamb in Revelation 5.

This development of images did not come to a halt with the end of the New Testament era. The well-known creedal and conciliar formulations from the fourth and fifth Christian centuries are another example. In their identification of Jesus with God, and as simultaneously "God and man," the early Church Fathers used ontological categories in the worldview of that epoch. A few years ago, I learned to assert the ultimate truth of Jesus in our contemporary context of relativism and pluralism by living in his story. More recently, I have written that "Grain of the Universe" functions as a contemporary equivalent of the biblical "Word" as an expression of the working of God in the world. With this book, Justin Heinzekehr suggests that we discuss Christology and the presence of God in the world in terms of ethical relationships developed in the absence of Christ materially present, as symbolized by the empty tomb. With this restatement, Heinzekehr joins a long tradition of expressing the meaning of Jesus by use of language and images from new and thus ever changing contexts.

It has been a pleasure to work with Justin Heinzekehr on this project as his ideas took shape. His attention to detail and his implementation of suggestions from anonymous reviewers and the editor are commendable. *The Absent Christ* is a worthy addition to the C. Henry Smith series. The book also bodes well for Heinzekehr's future in theological publication.

—*J. Denny Weaver, Editor, The C. Henry Smith Series*
Summer 2019

AUTHOR'S PREFACE

When I am asked to describe this book project to other people, and if these people seem to be expecting a response of only a few words, I tell them that I am revising my dissertation. That innocuous description is true, to be sure, but somewhat misleading. In reality this book, like all books, is a product of an evolution that goes much further back than anyone usually cares to trace. This simply reflects the normal fact that a book is really a slice of an ongoing conversation. But in this case there is even more reason than usual to add a caveat—the revisions to the original document are quite substantial. You find here completely new chapters and threads of thought that explore terrain not at all visible in the earlier dissertation. One might be justified in calling it a completely different book. To my mind, however, the core argument remains the same, with much of the technical material replaced by more rewarding extrapolations.

As near as I can tell, the beginnings of this project lie in a college course on Christian theology taught by Keith Graber Miller, which introduced me both to process theology and a variety of atonement theories, among which was J. Denny Weaver's nonviolent atonement. From the latter, I learned that Mennonite theology could have a distinct voice within the panoply of Christian attempts to answer life's big questions. At the same time, the "process" God was a new and challenging figure for me, but I was soon enchanted by the potential of a relational, empathic theology. My time in graduate studies at Claremont School of

Theology provided a wonderful environment to experiment with combinations of both of these interest areas.

As I think about the influences on this book, it is worth noting that in 2015, as much of this project was taking shape, Rachel Waltner Goossen published her analysis of John Howard Yoder's sexual abuse, using new documents that had come to light.[1] Along with Ruth Krall's *Elephant in God's Living Room*,[2] this article brought the status of Yoder's theology back into the forefront for many people engaged with Mennonite theology. Although Yoder's behavior toward women was already common knowledge, this was an additional opportunity for many of us to reflect on the future of Mennonite theology in light of feminist theology and the potential for sexual violence even within a pacifist denomination.

It is probably impossible to completely separate Yoder from contemporary Mennonite theology, but this book represents an attempt to articulate an alternative that takes into account, even at its foundations, issues of power dynamics and violence within faith communities. And so, although Yoder himself does not feature prominently here, the book should be understood as a response, albeit a negative one, to Yoder's ambiguous but profound theological legacy.

More positively, many faculty and students at Claremont helped deepen and complexify my understanding of theological nonviolence. I have to thank especially Roland Faber and Monica Coleman for serving on my dissertation committee and providing invaluable advice during that process. Philip Clayton was and continues to be an important mentor and friend, and our collaborative work on socialism and process philosophy turned out to have unanticipated connections to this project. Grace Kao, Richard Amesbury, Santiago Slabodsky, and Michael McGrath each made important contributions to my thinking which would be difficult to isolate, but which appear at crucial times throughout the book. Finally, I am deeply grateful for the often enlightening and always lively conversations with friends and peers at Claremont, especially Drew Baker.

Thanks to Duane Friesen for making suggestions and arranging for conversations with community members in North Newton, Kansas. Maxwell Kennell read the dissertation manuscript and has been an important conversation partner as a fellow Mennonite metaphysician. Part of the Introduction began as a sermon at Washington

Mennonite Church in Iowa, where I received good suggestions and feedback. Many of the themes in Chapter 2 appeared in a paper presentation at the Mennonite Scholars and Friends meeting at the American Academy of Religion in Atlanta. Chapter 6 was delivered as a paper at the 2017 Rooted and Grounded conference at Anabaptist Mennonite Biblical Seminary in Elkhart, Indiana. Many thanks to those who provided feedback and conversation over the course of those meetings.

A special thanks to J. Denny Weaver, who has been influential all along the way, as a supportive and encouraging presence, as a member of my dissertation committee, as a reader and editor, and as a valued teacher and friend.

Finally, my wife Hannah, a theologian in her own right, has been integral in conversations, editing, and suggesting changes to the manuscript, as well as entertaining our children when I had to make serious writing progress.

—*Justin Heinzekehr*

INTRODUCTION: THE VOICE OF THE MOST HIGH

This book traces a recurring theme in Christian theology. It has to do with the question of ultimate authority: how does the sacredness or divinity that we associate with Jesus, either as a human figure or a cosmological Christ, get translated to our actual, everyday reality? What difference does Christ make to our churches, our politics, our work, our education, our consumption? What kind of demand does Christ make upon us?

Traditionally, in Christian theology, the connection between world and God is the function of the sacrament; the sacrament is a symbol that expresses the translation of the sacred to the mundane. Therefore one might call this book an example of sacramental theology, though I suspect that label would hardly be a draw for most readers. Sacraments can bring to mind precisely the opposite movement that we are tracing here. They can be associated with an overly "metaphysical" religion, in which participants are directed away from their material, day-to-day concerns and granted a temporary spiritual existence, which sticks to them for a little while before wearing off with the bustle of everyday life.

The theme we are tracing in this book is the counter-theme to the "metaphysical" sacrament. One might call it the materialist, deconstructive, or liberative sacrament. Its function is to locate the sacred in concrete, material, everyday relations, in an inverse direction to lines of power that define these relations. Actually, this type of theology is just as metaphysical as any other theology, in that it deals with underlying patterns that characterize reality as a whole. It is "meta-physical" not in the sense that it seeks to escape physicality but that it provides broad principles for interpreting physicality.

Paradoxically, the symbol for a materialist sacramental theology has often been couched in terms of absence, as a gap or lacuna in the fabric of physical reality. It may be because the natural human tendency is to place the source of ultimate authority outside of the mundane, which necessitates the use of a placeholder or cipher to deflect the search for transcendence back down to earth. It may be that absence keeps our gaze from settling on a particular object of authority, preserving a dynamic, flowing orientation toward the world. At any rate, the primary symbol for our analysis is the absent Christ, which begins with the physical absence of Jesus' body at the empty tomb, extends to the unavailability of Christ as an objective, transcendent authority in the development of the early church, and even now contains social, political, and ecological implications for Christian theology.

The absent Christ can be described in a kind of dialectical movement that transitions from individual authority to communal authority to marginal authority. In the Christian narrative, one moves from the historical Jesus of the Gospels to the creation of the church of Acts to its expansion to the poor or disenfranchised. Many of us are more or less familiar with this narrative, and that arc remains the basic framework for this book.

A most elegant and concise presentation of the fundamental structure of absent divinity comes from a Talmudic story that tells of a disagreement among a group of rabbis, in which there is a clear transfer of divine authority from individual to community to marginalized.[3] So let us begin *not* with the story of the empty tomb, but with the story of Eliezer and the oven of Akhnai, which I include here more or less in full. It may seem, in a book on Christian theology, that we are beginning already with a digression—a bad sign, perhaps, for the rest of the book. I leave the reader to decide that point, but it seems to me that when one reconsiders such a familiar narrative as that of the empty tomb, it can be helpful to sneak up on it from an unexpected direction.

The Oven of Akhnai

It might be difficult for us to see the importance of the rabbis' disagreement now, but at the time it was very serious. The question concerned a new type of oven, called the oven of Akhnai, made of pieces of concrete surrounded by sand. Several rabbis had gathered to answer the question: does this type of oven get defiled when it touches something unclean? In Leviticus 11, for instance, it is said that if anything unclean, like an animal carcass, falls onto an oven, one has to break that oven up into pieces and never use it again. Obviously this could be quite inconvenient for anyone trying to cook a piece of meat.

Almost all the rabbis agreed that these stringent rules should apply to the oven of Akhnai. However, Rabbi Eliezer, the most charismatic and powerful of the group, was certain that the Scriptures made an exception. He believed that because these ovens were made of different pieces of clay with sand and mortar in between, they were not actually complete utensils; therefore the rules did not apply to them in the same way.

Now Eliezer was a crucial person in the community. In every single debate in the past, he had been proven right. He had even been known to work miracles and to be able to speak directly with heaven. Thus when the rabbis met to discuss how they should classify this oven, Rabbi Eliezer was sure that he would be able to convince the other rabbis of his position. He used every argument he could think of. He showed the rabbis exactly where the Torah supported his position and why this was the correct interpretation. Still the rest of the rabbis were not convinced.

Eventually Eliezer got so exasperated with their stubbornness that he pointed to a nearby carob tree and said, "If the Scriptures agree with me, let this carob tree prove it." And the carob tree uprooted itself, moved a hundred feet over the field, and sent roots down again. But the other rabbis replied, "No proof can be brought from a carob tree."

So Eliezer pointed to a river that was flowing by their meetinghouse. "If the Scriptures agree with me, let this river prove it." And as the rabbis watched, the river began to flow upstream, against its natural course. But the rabbis replied, "No proof can be brought from a river."

So Eliezer said, "If the Scriptures agree with me, let the very walls of this meetinghouse prove it." And the walls of the building where they were sitting began to tilt inward as if they were going to fall in on them.

Rabbi Joshua quickly stood up and said, "When the people of God are engaged in a dispute, what right do you have to interfere?" And the walls stopped at an angle out of respect to Rabbi Joshua.

Finally, Eliezer said, "If the Scriptures agree with me, let it be proved from heaven!"

And the rabbis heard a voice from heaven saying, "Why do you not listen to Rabbi Eliezer, who is always correct in his interpretation of Scripture?"

But Rabbi Joshua protested, "Our text is not in heaven. We pay no attention to a divine voice." Rabbi Eliezer was overruled, the majority voices became a consensus, and the Akhnai oven was burned.

Some time later, the prophet Elijah came down from heaven to talk to Rabbi Nathan. (This apparently caused no one any great surprise.) Nathan was curious what God thought about Rabbi Joshua's statement in that earlier meeting. "What did the Holy One do in that moment?" Nathan asked.

Elijah answered, "God laughed with joy, saying, 'My people have defeated me. My people have defeated me.'"

The point of the first half of the story is not so much about the specifics of the rabbis' disagreement. It's meant as a commentary on Deuteronomy 30:12, a verse which says, "[These commandments] are not in heaven. . . . No, the word is very near to you; it is in your mouth and in your heart for you to observe." To the rabbis, this meant that God had given their community authority to interpret Scripture and make decisions about how to apply it. Authority does not reside in charismatic individuals, or miraculous events, not even when someone claims to have access to a voice from heaven that supports his position. Authority does not even reside in a sacred text, at least not as an objective, independent text. The authority of the text comes from its interpretation, debate, and implementation in the context of a faith community.

The second half of the story, less often told, is actually the more important in terms of the dialectic of divine absence. Having come to a consensus, the rabbis burned the oven of Akhnai, along with all the other implements that Rabbi Eliezer had proclaimed clean in contradiction to the group. They decided to banish Eliezer to prevent future disagreements and to preserve the peace of their community. When Eliezer learned of the rabbis' decision, he tore his clothes and began to weep. And his distress caused all sorts of afflictions across the entire world: one third of the world's olives, wheat, and barley crops were destroyed. Dough that was being kneaded into bread spoiled, and everywhere that Eliezer turned his gaze was burned. At that very moment, Rabbi Gamaliel, who had presided over the decision to ostracize Eliezer, was traveling by boat, and a huge wave sprang up and threatened to engulf him. It was only by a timely prayer that Gamaliel was able to keep the boat from sinking.

Eliezer's wife, who also happened to be Gamaliel's sister, had seen the destructive results of Eliezer's grief, and supervised him constantly so that she could keep him from bowing his head in the traditional prayer of supplication, which would certainly produce new disasters.

But one day she left for a moment to deliver bread to a pauper outside the door, and when she came back she found Eliezer bowed in prayer. "You have killed my brother!" she cried, and indeed at that moment came the sound of a trumpet announcing the death of Rabbi Gamaliel.

"How did you know that your brother would die?" Eliezer asked.

She replied, "All the gates of heaven are apt to be locked, except for the gates of prayer for victims of mistreatment."

The stated moral of the second half of the story is that those who verbally mistreat others have violated the commandments. But when both halves are taken together, this story clearly has broader implications for communal authority: although one cannot derive authority from supernatural events or charismatic individuals, there is also the recognition that communal consensus can be abused to harm or suppress individuals. In the first case, the community is the locus of divine authority with respect to a powerful individual. In the second case, when the same individual is unfairly ostracized, divine authority flows away from the community. God is on the side of the rabbis when it is a question of an individual attempting to wield power over the community, but God listens to Eliezer when he is ostracized too harshly. God's presence is dependent on the relations of power that exist at any given time in the community.

Interpretations of Jesus

Although this is a Talmudic story, it highlights themes important to Christian theology as well. After all, as a first-century Jew, Jesus was thoroughly versed in the culture of textual debate. When he had his arguments with the Pharisees and gave his sermons on the law, he was engaging in a type of discourse that would later grow into both Rabbinic Judaism and early Christianity. And in some ways, Jesus seems to have been much like Rabbi Eliezer of this story. He was a charismatic teacher, inspiring stories of mass feedings, healings and miracles, calming storms. He appears to have felt an intimate relationship with God, praying as to a father. As early Christians later reflected on their experience, they realized that in Jesus, this teacher with whom they had spent three amazing years, they had seen the very face of God.

There were actually some early Christians who thought of Jesus primarily as a magician or miracle worker—in other words, a charismatic authority figure. Even up to the fifth century, a few early portraits of Jesus from Christian worship sites show him holding a magic wand, waving it over Lazarus or the paralytic, just as other Greco-Roman magicians would do.[4] For some Christians, Jesus was the one prayed to for personal miracles. If one needed some money, or was not been able to have children, Jesus was asked for these things. Even some early Christian gospels that did not make it into the New Testament portrayed Jesus as a sort of magician (the Infancy Gospel of Thomas, for example).

But as Christians continued to reflect on the significance of Jesus, the idea of Jesus as a charismatic authority figure or wonderworker ended up getting pushed to the periphery. Of course, we still remember Jesus' miracles, but the Gospels that became most significant for the church did not make these miracles the main purpose of Jesus' ministry. In fact, in John 16, Jesus says something that leads us in a very different direction from the magicians or even from Eliezer of the Talmudic story. He says, "Nevertheless I tell you the truth: it is to your advantage that I go away, for if I do not go away, the Advocate will not come to you; but if I go, I will send him to you."

Here John suggests that there is something valuable in the fact that the church had to develop in the absence of Jesus. In this interpretation, the authority that Jesus wielded during his historical ministry gets transferred to the church as a community of believers. This transition is symbolized in Pentecost, when the Spirit makes its first appearance, and continues in the accounts of the church councils in Acts. The church is now empowered to act in Jesus' name and make corporate decisions about the nature of the faith, just as the rabbis have the authority to interpret the law regardless of Eliezer's charismatic authority. In the Christian narrative, Christ does not remain in the character of charismatic individual, but is associated with the collective agency of the community. Here, Christ is better associated with the rabbis than with Eliezer.

But the last movement of the Talmudic story has Eliezer regaining a privileged relationship to divine authority, at the moment when he suffers unjust or overly harsh ostracism from the community, and this movement too parallels a certain interpretation of Christ *over against* the church in favor of the poor and oppressed. In this sense, Jesus' authority is not based on social power at all, whether individual or collective, but in solidarity with human suffering, precisely in an opposite direction to social power. There is an authority greater even than that of the faith community, an authority defined as that which is excluded by the norms and boundaries of the community.

The story of Eliezer traces the movement of authority or sacredness from a charismatic individual, to a communal consensus, and then to those who have been marginalized. And in Christian history, Jesus' absence allowed not only for the development of a community but a community that was oriented, at least ideally, to Jesus' presence in the hungry or thirsty, naked, sick, or imprisoned (Matt. 25). "Whoever welcomes [a child] in my name welcomes me," Jesus said (Matt. 18). Eventually, the disciples began to see Jesus all over the place: in the Gentiles who were eager to become part of their community, in an Ethiopian eunuch (Acts 8), in a fanatical Pharisee named Saul—all outsiders now seen to embody the demand of Christ. Paradoxically, it was only in Jesus' absence that the disciples could recognize the presence of the divine in these previously subordinate, ostracized or invisible populations.

Flows of Absence and Darkness

In Christian theology then, the flow of divinity is mediated by absence, especially absence in relation to communal power. Absence, of course, is difficult to grasp, difficult even to approach. Some mystics speak of a kind of darkness that vibrates with life. The "dark light" they call it, or sometimes the "dazzling darkness."[5] They realized that the journey toward God is not a journey toward greater clarity or understanding but a journey toward an impenetrable darkness. At times, this journey comes with feelings of discomfort and even abandonment. As we move closer to God, we feel God's presence slipping away from us until we are utterly alone in the void that pulses with mystery. But according to the mystics, what can at first feel like abandonment is actually the beginning of a more dynamic encounter with God. As we look into the void, we learn to see in a different way.

At its best, the church is a community that is not satisfied with its own decisions or identity, that instead helps to guide us into this mysterious, dazzling darkness. Only after we embrace absence do we realize that we can begin to find Jesus present again to us in strange places, in people that we never recognized before, especially the marginalized or suffering. Rather than seeking a transcendent authority in the heavens, we learn to look for divinity in the faces of those around us. In our neighbors, we finally hear the voice of Jesus speaking to us across the centuries in our own tongue. Jesus speaks again through the face of the hungry, sick or incarcerated ones, in all those who do not fit into the conventions of church and society.

We respond to Jesus by attending to each other and finding new communal responses to what we encounter. We not do these things because they are written in the Bible, although the biblical text can be an important resource for us as we decide how we will live together. We do not do these things because our leaders, whether political or ecclesial, have decided that they should be priorities for us, though leaders can help us articulate and explain our actions. The most urgent reason we work to create a dynamic, thriving community is that Jesus appears in the people around us.

Overview of This Book

This book has three main sections: the first two chapters trace the theme of the absent Christ historically, in the Gospels and the early church through the Reformation. The second section, chapters 3 and 4, abstracts from the historical use of the absent Christ to describe a theological and metaphysical framework. The last three chapters apply this framework to political theology, environmental ethics, and theories of nonviolence.

Chapter 1 argues that Christian theology has been from its beginnings a subjective task, requiring an interpretation of an experience or narrative in the absence of an authority figure that could guarantee a single meaning. Jesus' absence figures literally in the gospel accounts in the stories of the empty tomb but is also translated into theological principles such as kenosis, or rhetorical strategies such as *enargeia*. The absence at the heart of the Gospels is what grounds the liberatory trajectory of Christianity; it is in tension with the narratives of presence that grew up soon afterwards to control and domesticate the Christian message.

Chapter 2 follows the idea of the absent Christ to Luther and the Radical Reformation. Luther uses the idea of the absent God as leverage against the Medieval clerical system but opens the door for other interpretations of divine absence, like those of Zwingli, Calvin and the Anabaptists. Particularly in Balthasar Hubmaier's version of the Anabaptist sacraments, the absence of Christ helps ground a materialist Christianity, where salvation is bound up with ethical relationships in and across communities rather than an individual, subjective relationship to God.

Chapter 3 extends the insights of the Anabaptist sacrament to theology proper. If, according to Hubmaier, sacredness is mediated to the self within a relational matrix and in response to ethical demands, then the self must be conceived as a relational space shaped by social power. God, in turn, is the inverse space with respect to the self, the space that escapes being defined or contained by lines of power. As in Emmanuel Levinas' philosophy, God is represented by the Other, which cannot be expressed within the logic of the Self. God and the self fluctuate together based on the dynamics of social power, the self being constantly defined and redefined by the exercise of power, and God calling existing structures into question.

Chapter 4 introduces Alfred North Whitehead's metaphysics as a way of thinking about the absent Christ cosmologically. As in the previous chapter, the basic units of analysis are relations and events instead of independent substances. Whitehead, however, gives us language to express the relationship between God and the self as a cosmological pattern between God and the world. Especially in Catherine Keller's interpretation of process metaphysics, God is conceived as a spaciousness or absence which contains the demand for worldly responsiveness and creativity but without defining a specific future.

Chapter 5 compares two contemporary political theologians (Rene Girard and Paul Kahn) with the political theology implied by the absent Christ. Both authors connect the concept of sovereignty and sacrifice to the divine: political communities are maintained by the idea that the sovereign represents divine authority and can demand sacrifice from the members of that community. However, Girard and Kahn both miss the most revolutionary aspect of the Christian narrative. The sovereignty represented by the absent Christ is one that exists outside of the borders of the political community. Therefore, rather than attempting to escape the whole idea of sacredness (Girard) or attempting to broaden national sacredness to an international scope (Kahn), we should recognize sacredness as being located outside of political borders. God's demand calls us to serve, even in sacrificial ways, those who exist outside of the state.

Chapter 6 considers the difference that the theology of the absent Christ would make to environmental ethics. As a materialist theology, it has the potential to help us navigate between the twin pitfalls of anthropocentrism (making nature subservient to human interests) and romanticization (thinking of nature in ideal and ahistorical terms). If Hegel's view of nature reflects the Lutheran sacrament, the Anabaptist sacrament is best reflected in Marx's ecology, which calls for an unsentimental historical analysis of human relationships with the rest of the natural world.

Finally, chapter 7 outlines a theory of nonviolence based on the absent Christ. Using the idea of the self as a topographical space, the demand that Christianity makes upon us is to engage in creative "mapping" of our experience of the world to reveal gaps in social norms or structures. This is potentially an infinite activity, since maps can be drawn in infinite ways to highlight or hide an infinite number of real patterns. Nonviolence, then, is a commitment to a creative process of reevaluation, not a set of practices nor an achievement.

The recovery of the absent Christ as the center of the Christian experience is significant not only because it highlights the liberatory origins of Christianity, but also because it resists the temptation to turn liberation into self-justification. It has been too easy for well-meaning communities, particularly progressive communities, to adopt the language of liberation, or even put liberatory practices into place, and then assume that they have divine approval. One can all too easily point to symptoms of such overconfidence in churches, organizations, and political communities: a naïve trust in decision-making processes to guarantee an ethical outcome, too much emphasis on consensus as a bearer of truth, too much self-satisfaction with worship style or organizational culture. At its worst, this tendency can help mask undercurrents of abuse or exclusion.[6]

To recognize Christ as omni-absent is to recognize that the consensus of a community—that upon which everyone can agree—only captures what is irrelevant to that community. It can be useful to map irrelevance, certainly, but that activity in itself does not produce growth. It is the outliers that bear divine authority, not the mean. The relevant truth is always something hidden beyond the boundaries of consensus, something that cannot be expressed yet—but can perhaps be welcomed into speech under the right circumstances. The absent Christ is an invitation to an adventure, seldom comforting, often frightening, but in the end life-giving.

THE
ABSENT
CHRIST

ONE

THE CORDS OF THE GRAVE:
THE PRIMACY OF THE EMPTY TOMB

So let us carefully consider, brothers and sisters, out of what sort of material we have been fashioned, and who [we are] and as what sort of people we have come into the world, and out of what sort of tomb and darkness the one who formed and created us has led us into the world, having prepared in advance his benefactions before we were born.
—1 Clement 38:3[1]

Where do we begin when we begin doing theology? In Christian circles, perhaps especially Anabaptist circles, the safe answer is that we begin with Jesus. But that statement has come to be almost a truism. The real difficulty is to decipher what we mean by "beginning with Jesus." Even the most biblically based theologians face diverse portraits of Jesus: Does one privilege the Jesus who represents the royal line of David? The one who reaches out to women and the marginalized? The Jewish teacher of wisdom? The cosmic Christ? Then one also has to defend an interpretation of that portrait, which is always developed through the lens of some social context and philosophical commitment. Thus most anyone can lay claim to an authoritative or at least legitimate Christology, even as many are incompatible with each other.

Actually, the problem is that theology must always begin *without* Jesus. Despite all the efforts of the Jesus Seminar to pin down the identity of the historical person, there is no uncontroversial portrait of Jesus we can retrieve from the ravages of time. Even if there were—even if the "real" historical Jesus turned out to have been only a Palestinian prophet of the end times, and a mistaken one at that[2]—would it really invalidate all the theologies that have developed in very different directions since the first century? I would suggest not; the historical Jesus grounds but does not circumscribe theology. In fact, the power of Christianity is partly due to its flexibility, its tendency to adapt across cultures, to lend itself to new philosophies, to serve social movements. Christianity always happens in the middle of things, even at its beginning. So the absence in which Christianity develops is perhaps less a problem than a womb, a space allowing for theological artistry. Or if it *is* sometimes a problem, it is a problem we cannot afford to solve.

This chapter argues that the original Christian experience, the event most fundamental to its evolution as a unique religious movement, is in fact the experience of Jesus' absence at the empty tomb. Jesus' absence sparks the formation of a new kind of community in the context of that absence, and allows for the re-discovery of divine presence within that community. The Gospels do not present objective narratives about Jesus; rather, they are stories that helped organize various streams of half-conscious interpretations of Jesus so that they became relevant to the distinct communities who created them. What the Gospels have in common is their initiative to create meaning in the face of the absence of the original religious authority (Jesus the human). Thus in the Gospels we see the trace of Jesus' absence, and we should recognize this trace as the most basic characteristic of Christianity.

Origins of the Empty Tomb Narratives

Of course, the idea of divine absence long predates Christianity. The hidden God is a theme that runs throughout the Hebrew Bible. Sometimes God's absence is a metaphor for the suffering of Israel. Many psalms plead with God not to hide from the petitioner (Ps. 27, 44, 69, 102, etc.).[3] Similarly the prophetic books use God's absence to signify a suffering usually alleviated by a promise of future presence:

> For a brief moment I abandoned you,
> but with great compassion I will gather you.
> In overflowing wrath for a moment
> I hid my face from you,

but with everlasting love I will have compassion on you,
says the Lord, your Redeemer. (Isa. 54:7-8)

In the Deuteronomic tradition, God's absence is a strategy to deal with a disobedient people:

The Lord said to Moses, "Soon you will lie down with your ancestors. Then this people will begin to prostitute themselves to the foreign gods in their midst, the gods of the land into which they are going; they will forsake me, breaking my covenant that I have made with them. My anger will be kindled against them on that day. I will forsake them and hide my face from them; they will become easy prey, and many terrible troubles will come upon them. On that day they will say, 'Have not these troubles come upon us because our God is not in our midst?' On that day I will surely hide my face on account of all the evil they have done by turning to other gods." (Deut. 31:16-18)

But in another more significant sense, God gradually *becomes* absent through the traditions that make up the Hebrew Bible. Richard Friedman points out that the earliest texts of the Hebrew Bible portray God as intimately related to humans. God talks to the people, does public miracles, appears (however briefly) to Israelite leaders. This intimacy gradually gives way to a more distant or even ambiguous picture of God: the terrifying God of Job or the vague oversight God provides in Ezra and Nehemiah. In the book of Esther, God is not mentioned at all.[4] The process culminates in later Judaism, where the direct presence of God is translated into the authority of rabbinic debate, as illustrated by the story of the Oven of Akhnai in the Introduction.

In a related way, early Christians used Hebrew conceptions of divine absence when interpreting the significance of Jesus. There was no Christian writing before Jesus' death— "Christianity" did not exist while Jesus was alive. It was only in the face of Jesus' absence that his followers were forced to reflect on the identity and status of their movement, as something perhaps distinct from previous forms of Judaism. And so when people began to articulate a specifically Christian story and write it down in the form of gospels, the experience of the death and resurrection of Jesus took center stage.

As evident below, the narratives of the empty tomb appear in all four canonical gospels, a privilege shared only with Jesus' baptism, the

Mark 16	Matthew 28	Luke 24	John 20
1 When the Sabbath was over, Mary Magdalene, and Mary the mother of James, and Salome bought spices, so that they might go and anoint him. 2 And very early on the first day of the week, when the sun had risen, they went to the tomb. 3 They had been saying to one another, 'Who will roll away the stone for us from the entrance to the tomb?' 4 When they looked up, they saw that the stone, which was very large, had already been rolled back. 5 As they entered the tomb, they saw a young man, dressed in a white robe, sitting on the right side; and they were	1 After the Sabbath, as the first day of the week was dawning, Mary Magdalene and the other Mary went to see the tomb. 2 And suddenly there was a great earthquake; for an angel of the Lord, descending from heaven, came and rolled back the stone and sat on it. 3 His appearance was like lightning, and his clothing white as snow. 4 For fear of him the guards shook and became like dead men. 5 But the angel said to the women, 'Do not be afraid; I know that you are looking for Jesus who was crucified. 6 He is not here; for he has been raised, as he said.	1 But on the first day of the week, at early dawn, they came to the tomb, taking the spices that they had prepared. 2 They found the stone rolled away from the tomb, 3 but when they went in, they did not find the body. 4 While they were perplexed about this, suddenly two men in dazzling clothes stood beside them. 5 The women were terrified and bowed their faces to the ground, but the men said to them, 'Why do you look for the living among the dead? He is not here, but has risen. 6 Remember how he told you, while he was still in Galilee, 7 that the Son of man must be handed	1 Early on the first day of the week, while it was still dark, Mary Magdalene came to the tomb and saw that the stone had been removed from the tomb. 2 So she ran and went to Simon Peter and the other disciple, the one whom Jesus loved, and said to them, 'They have taken the Lord out of the tomb, and we do not know where they have laid him.' 3 Then Peter and the other disciple set out and went toward the tomb. 4 The two were running together, but the other disciple outran Peter and reached the tomb first. 5 He bent down to look in and saw the linen wrappings

alarmed. 6 But he said to them, 'Do not be alarmed; you are looking for Jesus of Nazareth, who was crucified. He has been raised; he is not here. Look, there is the place they laid him. 7 But go, tell his disciples and Peter that he is going ahead of you to Galilee; there you will see him, just as he told you.' 8 So they went out and fled from the tomb, for terror and amazement had seized them; and they said nothing to anyone, for they were afraid. [And all that had been commanded them they told briefly to those around Peter. And afterwards Jesus himself sent out through them, from east to west, the

Come, see the place where he lay. 7 then go quickly and tell his disciples, "He has been raised from the dead, and indeed he is going ahead of you to Galilee; there you will see him." This is my message for you. 8 So they left the tomb quickly with fear and great joy, and ran to tell his disciples. 9 Suddenly Jesus met them and said, 'Greetings!' And they came to him, took hold of his feet, and worshipped him. 10 Then Jesus said to them, 'Do not be afraid; go and tell my brothers to go to Galilee; there they will see me.'

over to sinners, and be crucified, and on the third day rise again.' 8 then they remembered his words, 9 and returning from the tomb, they told all this to the eleven and to all the rest. 10 Now it was Mary Magdalene, Joanna, Mary the mother of James, and the other women with them who told this to the apostles. 11 But these words seemed to them an idle tale, and they did not believe them. 12 But Peter got up and ran to the tomb; stooping and looking in, he saw the linen cloths by themselves; then he went home, amazed at what had happened.

lying there, but he did not go in. 6 then Simon Peter came, following him, and went into the tomb. He saw the linen wrappings lying there, 7 and the cloth that had been on Jesus' head, not lying with the linen wrappings but rolled up in a place by itself. 8 Then the other disciple, who reached the tomb first, also went in, and he saw and believed; 9 for as yet they did not understand the Scripture, that he must rise from the dead. 10 Then the disciples returned to their homes. 11 But Mary stood weeping outside the tomb. As she wept, she bent over to look into the tomb; [12]and she saw two angels in white, sitting where the body of Jesus had been lying, one at the head and the other at the feet. [13]They said to her, 'Woman, why are you weeping?' She said to them, 'They have taken away my Lord, and I do not know where they have laid him.' [14]When she had said this, she turned round and saw Jesus standing there, but she did not know that it was Jesus. [15]Jesus said to her, 'Woman, why are you weeping? For whom are you looking?' Supposing him to be the gardener, she said to him, 'Sir, if you have carried him away, tell me where you have laid him, and I will

sacred and imperishable proclamation of eternal salvation.]

take him away.'

[16]Jesus said to her, 'Mary!' She turned and said to him in Hebrew, 'Rabbouni!' (which means 'Teacher'). [17]Jesus said to her, 'Do not hold on to me, because I have not yet ascended to the Father. But go to my brothers and say to them, "I am ascending to my Father and your Father, to my God and your God."' [18]Mary Magdalene went and announced to the disciples, 'I have seen the Lord'; and she told them that he had said these things to her.

feeding of the multitude, and the rest of the passion narrative (in which the empty tomb is the climax). In the earliest version of the earliest gospel, Mark, the empty tomb is the final word of the entire story; the "appearance narratives" of the resurrected Jesus are later elaborations.

The stories of the empty tomb represent the early Christian memories of the development of the church in the period after Jesus' death, and provide some of the rationale for the transference of divine authority from Jesus to the Christian community,[5] not as a hierarchical lineage through which orthodoxy is passed down but as a constellation of communities empowered to interpret Jesus in and for their particular contexts.[6] In that sense the Gospels should be read backward, beginning with the absence of Jesus, which then elicits a contextual interpretation of the significance of Jesus' life. That absence provides a "grammar" for the Gospels,[7] within which a multitude of interpretations can be expressed. And so we miss the point when we read the Gospels as historical accounts. They are rather expositions of a new theological language, each centered on the existential problems and concerns of specific communities.

The gospels agree that a group of women made the initial discovery of the empty tomb, although as time progressed, the male disciples tended to play more of a role in the story. In the Synoptic gospels, at least, these are also stories about Jesus' absence; the figures that appear to the women are either angels (Matt.) or unspecified messengers (Mark and Luke). Even in John, there is an implied distance between Jesus and Mary that cannot be overcome ("do not hold on to me"/ "do not touch me").

Some scholars suggest that there were originally two sets of accounts of Jesus' resurrection, one that emphasized the appearance of Jesus to the disciples and one that emphasized the empty tomb. Daniel Smith argues that the empty tomb narratives were the primary material from which later narratives of resurrection and post-mortem appearances were constructed. Early Christian theologians found it necessary to control the problematic "disappearance" tradition, which allowed for a multiplicity of interpretations. So the appearance narratives tended to be used to establish apostolic authority, whereas the absence narratives tended to democratize authority.[8] For example, Paul quotes an appearance tradition in 1 Corinthians 15 to bolster his own reliability:[9]

[H]e appeared to Cephas, then to the twelve. Then he appeared to more than five hundred brothers and sisters at one time, most of whom are still alive, though some have died. Then he appeared to James, then to all the apostles. Last of all, as to one untimely born, he appeared also to me. (1 Cor. 15:5-8)

Whereas Paul's articulation of the Christian kerygma is ordered around clear lines of masculine authority, the empty tomb narratives are connected with the women who witness the tomb and say that Jesus has gone ahead of them to Galilee (Mark 16:7).

Elisabeth Schüssler Fiorenza suggests that the mention of Galilee signifies Jesus' location in a particular context of struggle, his presence in the "ekklesia of wo/men gathered in Jesus' name."[10] Jesus is no longer simply present, but he is also not merely located in some transcendent heaven. Jesus now appears in the resistance of a particular community to injustice and violence. Perhaps counterintuitively, the empty tomb narratives resist the assumption of authority by individual male leaders precisely because of Jesus' absence; they allow for Jesus' authority to be claimed by those struggling for liberation of some kind.

Emptiness as Kenosis

The absence of Jesus becomes not only a negative space in which Christian communities project their own authority. It also becomes an early christological principle, something inherent about Jesus' identity. This is most obvious in the idea of *kenosis*, apparently part of an early hymn that Paul references in Philippians 2:

Let the same mind be in you that was in Christ Jesus, who, though he was in the form of God, did not regard equality with God as something to be exploited, but emptied himself, taking the form of a slave, being born in human likeness. And being found in human form, he humbled himself and became obedient to the point of death—even death on a cross. (Phil. 2:5-8)

As Sarah Coakley points out, kenosis can take on many different meanings in traditional Christian discourse. One can emphasize Christ's relinquishment of power, either temporarily (as cosmic redeemer) or in appearance only (as gnostic redeemer).[11] Under these interpretations, kenosis is linked most closely with incarnation; the important point is that a pre-existing Christ gave up his divinity to take human form.

But Coakley argues it is more likely that this passage originally had a more ethical meaning: that Jesus was created in "the form of God," like Adam in the Genesis account and that, unlike Adam, Jesus carried out his ministry as a servant instead of grasping for power. (The Christian doctrine of the pre-existence of Christ was based on later speculation, for instance, in Justin Martyr of the second century.[12]) Under Coakley's interpretation, then, kenosis is related more to Jesus' life and ministry, and especially his willingness to suffer rather than to assume power.[13]

This interpretation can be extended to a metaphysical claim: that Jesus reveals the character of God to be very different than worldly conceptions of power.[14] The context in which Paul uses the hymn bears out Coakley's interpretation: Paul is encouraging his readers to act compassionately and consider the needs of others in their community. Kenosis, as Paul uses the term, represents God's act of solidarity with us and, as we accept Jesus' mindset as our own, our act of solidarity with others.[15]

Though the term "kenosis" is used only in Philippians, the same concept of self-emptying service is found throughout the Gospels. In Luke, for instance, we see a kenotic movement first in Mary's Magnificat, where God "has looked with favor on the lowliness of his servant" (Luke 1:48). Juan Marin says:

> The angel's prophecy to Mary about Christ's enthronement would then involve a reversal of the roles between the mighty and the meek, that in the hymn serve as basis for the linguistic interplay between emptiness and fullness. Those who are arrogant are brought down from their thrones and the humility of the downtrodden exalted. Those emptied of everything are filled. Those who are haughty, rich, and "full of themselves" are sent away empty.[16]

Luke's narrative of Jesus' ministry continues to highlight this dynamic rhythm of emptiness and fullness: the bridegroom who seats his slaves and serves them food (12:37), Jesus' instructions to the disciples to act as servants (22:24-27), and the cup "poured out for you" as a new covenant (22:20).[17]

The absence of Jesus at the tomb (and later at the ascension) therefore goes hand in hand with Luke's broader kenotic Christology.

Christ's kenosis requires his disappearance so that the disciples do not reduce the kerygma to his image, confuse the logos with the *dialogismoi*, or confuse the Word with words—with those thoughts and reasonings Mary and Christ perceive in the hearts of the proud. The message is to search for him instead in the "image of a human being," which he took in kenosis.[18]

Jesus' self-emptying is here not self-negation or submission; it signifies Jesus' resistance to the tendency to grasp at power. Through Jesus' emptiness, the disciples are able to search for truth in the concrete encounter with human others, especially those at the margins of society. Jesus is unavailable as an authority figure who can safeguard a single, orthodox interpretation of truth.[19] The discovery of the empty tomb is therefore a seminal point in the formation of the early church.[20] The experience of emptiness allows for the "pouring out" of the Spirit at Pentecost—the empowerment of the church to interpret and carry on Jesus' mission in his absence.

Emptiness as *Enargeia*

The absence of the empty tomb is not portrayed as a simple absence; it is a living absence, an absence that carries the trace of presence.[21] This description might seem more paradoxical to modern readers than it would have to the original audience of the Gospels. The concept of *enargeia*—"absent presence"—was a familiar one in first-century rhetorical theory. Though the term does not appear in the New Testament, classical rhetoricians recognized that speech had the power to create vivid impressions in the listeners, almost as if the things being spoken of were immediately present. Dionysius of Halicarnassus describes the phenomenon as such:

> [*Enargeia*] is a certain power of conveying the things being spoken of to the senses, and it comes from his grasp of circumstantial details. No one who applies his mind to Lysias' words will be so awkward, so difficult to please or so slow-witted as not to suppose that he is seeing the things being presented actually happening and that he is face-to-face in the company of the people the orator introduces as if they were present.[22]

The successful orator or writer uses *enargeia* to create a "time shift," making the past present once again to the audience.[23] They do this by activating specific memories that the audience shares, or through the use of sensory images and details that lend vividness to a narration. "With his command of rhetorical techniques the orator is able to create *phantasiai* or *visiones*, that is: imaginary scenes. These present the verbal utterance of a *narratio* in such a way that the event described seems to be happening *hic et nunc* before the inner eye of the recipient."[24] If it is successful, the effect of enargeia is such that "the text opens up to the reader's imagination: the words on the page dissolve into images as they impact upon the mind."[25]

Enargeia was not only about presenting an objective portrayal of a past event; it had connotations of passion and desire. Lucretius, for instance, discusses "the paradoxes of erotic absent presence . . . 'for if the object of your love is absent, yet images of it are present and the sweet name sounds in your ears,' where ocular and verbal representations conjure up the absent beloved."[26] By playing on the gap between the real absence of a person or event and its vivid presence in the imaginations of the audience, the orator is able to produce not only an awareness of facts, but an erotic pull toward the reality to which they refer. In Aelius Aristides' oration on the destruction of Smyrna, for example, "the gap between Smyrna's remembered glory and current desolation is intended to stir the audience to long for it as it had been."[27] A successful use of enargeia thus makes a specific affective claim on the audience; it is above all else a mode of persuasion toward a particular emotional state.

Jane Heath argues that Paul's description of the *parousia* in 1 Thessalonians 1-3 draws on this ancient understanding of enargeia to make the hoped-for return of Christ vividly present to the Thessalonian church. "Enargeia, the sense of vivid presence of that as yet absent parousia, is experienced in seeing one another. . . . Just as enargeia was appreciated for its *truth/reality* value, so this imbues the hope in the parousia with a sense of its reality. It persuades. It thus strengthens faith."[28]

Insofar as the concept of enargeia was part of the Greco-Roman assumptions about reading texts, we might also expect to find it in the Gospels. The opening of Luke's gospel, for instance, exhibits many of the ideals of enargeia: drawing on shared memories to produce an account of a past event, no longer accessible to the reader, that is so truthful, vivid and persuasive that the reader becomes essentially an eyewitness.[29]

The concept of enargeia, I would suggest, was given an even more radical interpretation by the early Christians. Rather than referring to a merely imagined presence, the early Christians came to understand that the absent Jesus could be truly present to them as mediated through human others. Perhaps the strongest statement of this intuition comes in the parable of the sheep and the goats in Matthew 25:

> Then the righteous will answer him, "Lord, when was it that we saw you hungry and gave you food, or thirsty and gave you something to drink? And when was it that we saw you a stranger and welcomed you, or naked and gave you clothing? And when was it that we saw you sick or in prison and visited you?" And the king will answer them, "Truly I tell you, just as you did it to one of the least of these who are members of my family, you did it to me."

Here the memory of Jesus' ministry to the disenfranchised creates in the early Christian community a kind of *enargeic* sensitivity to those around them. Through Jesus' absence, the early Christians understood the call of their neighbors to be a sort of speech making Jesus vivid to them again, not only as a memory but as a real presence that creates a pull or a demand upon them.

The gospel narratives of the empty tomb thus give witness to the early Christian experience of Jesus as a vacated authority-space. It is precisely this space that allows for the formation of a community that is empowered to interpret truth in its own context, out of a response to the needs that it encounters both within and outside of its own borders. It explicitly undermines the idea of Christ as providing a stable, reified truth (i.e., one that could be codified as "orthodoxy") in favor of Christ as an absence who pulls the community into relationship with human others to construct creative interpretations that are "articulated and proven 'right' again and again within the continuing struggles for survival, justice, and well-being."[30]

In this sense Christ functions as a Levinasian "trace," which is never graspable but makes some sort of difference to the one who attempts to follow it. The community does not find Christ through an objective analysis of Scripture, nor by unearthing a historical personality, but through the "faces" of those in and around the community.[31] The significance of the Gospels' "he is not here"[32] is that one cannot locate or define Christ in any concrete way that would insulate one from the contingent and particular relations of one's community.

The revolutionary potential of Jesus' absence could sometimes be domesticated as Christianity spread across the empire, developed institutions, made political alliances, and struck compromises with social mores. However, it has always reemerged from time to time, usually accompanying anti-establishment social movements. The next chapter explores the role of the absent Christ in an especially anti-establishment era: the Protestant Reformation. Divine absence was a theme for many of the reformers, and other authors have traced its effect on modern science, secularism, and democracy. However, I focus particularly on the "Radical Reformation," the Anabaptists, who took Christ's absence furthest toward a communal Christian ethic.

TWO

FOUNDATIONS LAID BARE: RADICAL RE-FORMATION

It follows that [Christ] is not present. For if he were present, then we would hold the Supper in vain and against the words of Christ and Paul. For where a person is essentially and bodily present, there a remembrance is not necessary. However, where he is not bodily present, then one celebrates his remembrance until he comes.
—Balthasar Hubmaier

The idea of divine absence resurfaces in Christian theology, often in times and places where it is necessary to articulate some alternative to institutional orthodoxy. As noted in the Introduction, mystics tend to be great theologians of absence. Gregory of Nyssa describes the incomprehensible God who can only be approached in darkness, where true knowledge is a "seeing that consists in not seeing."[1] John of the Cross speaks of the "dark night of the soul," in which the believer experiences a profound absence. Julian of Norwich describes an overwhelming sense of being "left alone."[2] But in Christian mysticism, as in the Gospel stories of the empty tomb, divine absence is not simply a blank but a means toward a deeper sort of presence, usually one that can be achieved directly and personally rather than through an institutional hierarchy.[3]

It should not be surprising, then, that a similar theology of absence occurs in the Reformation, which can be seen as the culmination of a long-simmering anti-institutionalism in late medieval Europe. The *deus absconditus*, or hidden God, was a major theme in Luther's writing, and later reformers adopted the idea in different ways. For the reformers, too, divine hiddenness or absence functions as a way of reaffirming and renegotiating human access to the divine. But each of the reform movements that sprang up after Luther used divine absence to point toward different kinds of presence. Our task in this chapter is to trace the idea of theological absence from the roots of the Reformation through its most radical expression in the "left wing" Anabaptist movements. Here, I would suggest, the ethical implications of divine absence were most fully developed.

The Triumph of Nominalism

In Europe, the fourteenth century was a particularly fruitful time for mysticism as well as for a new philosophical school called nominalism. It would be an understatement to call this a tumultuous time. The bubonic plague killed somewhere between a third and a half of the population. England and France were in the middle of the disastrous Hundred Years' War. The Crusades had failed, dealing a major blow to the assumption of Christian Europe's superiority. As a result, many Europeans began to question the idea of an unchanging social and natural order, which had been popular in scholastic philosophy up to that point. Previously, most theologians had assumed that God was reflected in the natural order, that the world conformed to a divine logic that could be grasped intellectually. But for nominalist philosophers, the world seemed to be much more chaotic and unpredictable, and God much more distant and mysterious.

William of Ockham (1287-1347) is often given credit for starting the "nominalist revolution."[4] He argued, against the scholastics, that God was actually not bound by any kind of logic at all. God was unpredictable and unknowable.

> [T]he God that nominalism revealed was no longer the beneficent and reasonably predictable God of scholasticism. The gap between man and God had been greatly increased. God could no longer be understood or influenced by human beings—he acted simply out of freedom and was indifferent to the consequences of his acts. He laid down rules for human conduct, but he might

change them at any moment. Some were saved and some were damned, but there was only an accidental relation between salvation and saintliness, and damnation and sin. It is not even clear that this God loves man. The world this God created was thus a radical chaos of utterly diverse things in which humans could find no point of certainty or security.[5]

Ockham's philosophy has many important implications that shape our modern world: the distancing of God from the material and political world, the necessity of empirical methods of study, the possibility of radical human freedom. The nominalist God is inaccessible, hidden to human understanding and forecasting. Because nominalism helped to undermine the inevitability of the medieval ecclesial and political structures, the "absence" of the nominalist God created an environment in which the Reformation could become an attractive and compelling movement. If these power structures of society were not divinely ordained, then they were open to change.

By the sixteenth century, nominalism had become increasingly popular. The medieval social order continued to crumble and the ecclesial and political hierarchies that had existed for more than a millennium seemed now much less inevitable and therefore more oppressive. Of course, there had been many challenges to this social order in late medieval society; the Renaissance humanists had called for reform and certain communities of dissenting Christians like the Lollards and Waldensians had already broken away from papal authority. In the Reformation, however, the criticism of the dominant social order intensified and broadened. Whereas most of the criticism before the Reformation came from within the church and was gradualist in character, critics in the Reformation sought to abolish the clerical system altogether.[6]

Despite the colorful accusations from reformers, the phenomenon of anticlericalism was probably not caused by an actual increase in clerical corruption; rather, it developed out of a long tradition of anticlerical rhetoric before the Reformation and was exacerbated by the rise of nominalism.[7] The Reformation was therefore a function of growing dissatisfaction with the power structures that characterized late medieval society as a whole—economically, religiously, and intellectually.[8]

This anti-establishment energy, once released, was not easy to contain. There were groups of people who wanted to take the reforms that Luther advocated further than he himself was comfortable with. Historians lump these people into the category of "Radical Reformation," though in reality they represented a diverse set of agenda and were not always compatible with one another.[9]

The Eucharist as Political Debate

During the Reformation, the sacraments (especially baptism and the Eucharist) became the main symbolic vehicle for disagreements between reforming movements. The sacramental debates may seem to modern readers to be arcane and petty disputes about abstract metaphysical concepts. It is hard for us to imagine getting worked up about an argument over the symbolic or real nature of the bread and wine. In the Reformation, however, these questions generated not only insults and profanity but also arrests and executions. In that era, the Eucharist was the primary way of understanding how God was made present or remained absent to the world, just as in early Christianity, questions of divine presence and absence functioned as a way to draw lines of religious and political power. The language of the Eucharist thus became a vehicle for broader disagreements about identity, culture and social institutions. (To put it in contemporary context, we might compare it to the vitriol that sexuality or gun control generate as symbols of a broader cultural divide in modern American Christianity.) Thus it was important to establish just how God was or was not present in the Eucharist.

It was Martin Luther who reintroduced the concept of *deus abconditus*, or the hidden God, into Reformation theology, but it had appeared in Scholastic philosophy as well. Thomas Aquinas used the term to refer to the aspects of God that transcended human understanding. However, in Scholastic philosophy, the hidden God can be approached via analogy. We may not be able to grasp the full nature of God, but we can, for example, know something about divine goodness by looking at finite human goodness. In this way of thinking, the difference between God and humans is one of scale. The human capability pales in comparison to the reality of God, but the comparison can be made nonetheless.[10]

Before the Reformation, then, the structures of the church could be seen as containing real theological information; the church mirrored and mediated the divine to the average person. The Eucharist could therefore be understood as an objective event. During the mass, the elements are transubstantiated into the body and blood of Christ, and they have an automatic spiritual effect on the participants in the mass. In other words, it does not matter what the mindset is of the one who eats the bread and drinks the wine, nor does it matter whether or not the priest is a good priest, God is made present through a hierarchical structure ordained by God, and one has access to God by participating in the divine order.

When Luther used the term *deus absconditus*, he meant something quite different, essentially taking the path that earlier nominalist philosophers had opened in contrast to the Scholastic view. For Luther, it is not the case that God can be understood, even theoretically, by an extension of logic or reason. Rather, God's revelation occurs precisely *in* God's obscurity. God appears most clearly in the event of the crucifixion, an event that breaks human understanding altogether. Alister McGrath describes Luther's theology as follows:

> Both the *Deus absconditus* and *Deus revelatus* are to be found precisely in the same event of revelation: which of the two is recognized depends on the perceiver. For example, consider the wrath of God revealed in the cross. To reason, God thus appears wrathful; to faith, God's mercy is revealed in this wrath. There is no question of God's mercy being revealed independently of his wrath, or of an additional and subsequent revelation of God's mercy which contradicts that of his wrath.[11]

In his later work, Luther pushes the idea of the hidden God even further. In his debates with Erasmus, for instance, Luther says that God has an even deeper hidden nature that may contradict the revealed God (which itself can only be grasped by faith). In other words, God is hidden not only *in* Christ but also *apart from* Christ. This is usually related to the doctrine of double predestination, where God assigns some people to salvation and others to damnation.[12]

In the Eucharist, however, God's grace is made present to the believer. But instead of relying on the mediation of the church, Luther suggested that the grace of God is given directly to the individual. There is nothing a Christian can do to achieve perfection but to turn toward God and accept the free gift of salvation. Therefore, for Luther the transference of the sacred to the world was partly subjective; it depended on the state of mind of the individual. In fact, there was no way to tell outwardly if a person had received grace or not. The Eucharist, then, is not automatically effective, nor does it depend on the priestly office or position in the ecclesial hierarchy. For Luther, as in the Catholic mass, the elements are identified with the real presence of Christ, but the objective elements require a subjective response to be effective.

Luther's concept of divine absence was key to his break from the Catholic church, but later reformers would take the idea even further. In particular, Andreas Karlstadt and Ulrich Zwingli held that Christ was absent even in the Eucharist. Rather than being a vehicle for Christ's presence, the Eucharist is meant to be a memorial rather than a physical event. Christ is spiritually present in each believer, but the elements themselves are only a sign of this psychological presence. For Zwingli, the bread and the wine are merely physical symbols that point to a change in the participants themselves. The Eucharist makes Christ present not in the elements, but in the members of the church.[13] The social significance of this change was to encourage democratic tendencies and criticisms of the clerical establishment. In Luther's thinking, Zwingli was taking things too far in the direction of decentralization:

> [Zwingli's] position was very similar to that taught by the Zwickau prophets and adopted by Karlstadt during Luther's exile at Wartburg, and Luther seems to have associated a symbolic understanding of the Eucharist with the political unrest that accompanied Karlstadt's reforms of 1521-1522. So he proved to be singularly unwilling to compromise with Zwingli over the proper understanding of the Eucharist.[14]

In other words, the debates over the Eucharist were debates over social power. To what extent could individuals claim divine authority independent of the rituals and establishment of the church? The Reformation opened a continuum from centralized to decentralized social authority, and where one fell on this continuum was expressed by the degree to which God was present or absent in one's sacramental theology.

Zwingli's sacramental theology would be a significant influence on Calvin, although Zwingli laid much more stress on the absence of Christ, whereas Calvin emphasized the spiritual presence of Christ within the church.[15] Zwingli's theory was significant because it moved the Eucharist from being an individual event (God is mediated to the participant via the elements) to a corporate event. However, in the Zwinglian and, later, Calvinist view, it is still a mainly psychological process; that is, God is mediated to the believer in the form of an inward transformation. Certainly, the church should demonstrate a transformation that includes mutual care and service, but the main purpose of the sacrament is to strengthen one's inner faith: "You do inwardly what you represent outwardly, your soul being strengthened by the faith which you attest in tokens."[16]

Hubmaier's Eucharist

In the Anabaptist movement, divine absence was carried furthest toward a democratized and materialized ecclesiology. Balthasar Hubmaier, the only Anabaptist leader with formal theological training, developed a theory of the Lord's Supper that built on Zwingli's but was ultimately distinct from it. Like Zwingli, Hubmaier was reacting against the Lutheran (and Catholic) idea of the real presence, whereby the Eucharistic elements become an actual location of Christ. Unlike Zwingli, however, Hubmaier believed that the change effected by the Eucharist required an external component; it is effective only in an ethical response of love between participants and to others beyond the church.

In Hubmaier's view, the transformation of the congregation at the time of the Eucharist is more than just symbolic.[17] When the participants come together with the desire to extend love to one another, there is an ontological shift: the church really becomes the body of Christ.[18] Although Christ is in an important sense absent from the Eucharist, the church makes Christ physically present in the world as they carry out Christ's teachings.[19]

Hubmaier uses the bread and the wine as the most important analogy for this transformation that occurs in Christian community. In his "Theses Concerning the Mass," he says,

> We all are one bread and one body—we all, who have fellowship in one bread and in one drink. As one little kernel does not keep its own flour, but shares it with others, and a single grape does not keep its juice for itself, but shares it with the others, so should we Christians also act—or we eat and drink unworthily from the table of Christ.[20]

Here the image of selfhood is almost that of absorption into a whole—the speck of flour into a loaf, or a drop of juice into a cup. The movement of the Eucharist here appears to be the merging of individual identity into the corporate body.

This would not be quite accurate, however, because Hubmaier is always careful to differentiate Christ, whose "particular place" is "in heaven" and is therefore absent from the elements and from any other created thing,[21] and the church, which somehow embodies Christ but always remains distinct from him. The breaking of the bread then symbolizes the self-sharing nature of Christ, a relationship that does not negate or diminish the self, nor merge individuals into a single entity.

This is, in fact, a result of Hubmaier's rejection of Catholic transubstantiation and of Zwingli's symbolic interpretation; the complete absence of Christ in the Eucharist allows him to conceive of a relational universe in which individuals are both ontologically distinct from one another and also communicate and embody important aspects of each other's very being.[22] In other words, Christian identity or selfhood is produced by and emerges from material *relations* rather than being based on an independent object, whether substantial or psychological.

When Hubmaier discusses the breaking of the bread, then, he not only draws on connotations of oneness or wholeness but also fragmentation or dissemination. As MacGregor says,

> When the church consumes the one loaf, of which each member of the church eats a fragment, the unified church shares in the nature of the one physical body of Christ, in which each member comprises a unique "little kernel" (*kernlin*).[23]

The breaking of the bread signifies both the method by which Christ becomes available to the church, and the method by which the members of the church have pledged to make themselves available to others. It signifies the willingness to make others, especially vulnerable others, an intimate and at times costly part of one's own identity:

> We conclude that the bread and wine of the Christ meal are outward word symbols of an inward Christian nature here on earth, in which a Christian obligates himself to another in Christian love with regard to body and blood. Thus as the body and blood of Christ became my body and blood on the cross, so likewise shall my body and blood become the body and blood of my

neighbor, and in time of need theirs become my body and blood, or we cannot boast at all to be Christians.[24]

So, when an officiant says the words, "This is my body, broken for you," Hubmaier would have us interpret it as referring to the church's commitment to shattering our simple individual identities in favor of multifaceted identities that depend on who we encounter and how we respond. From an Anabaptist perspective, there is no Christian identity that exists before and apart from one's relationships or community.

Implications of Divine Absence

In each of the Reformation theologies, the idea of divine absence plays a key role in articulating where and how God enters into the world. In general, God's absence is used as leverage to pry power away from some authority structure and redistribute that sacredness. For Luther, God's absence means that God is inaccessible through the hierarchy of the church, but is present to the individual through the elements. For Zwingli and Calvin, God is absent from the elements themselves (and therefore from the officiants), but present psychologically to the church community. For Hubmaier, finally, God is absent even from the community per se, but becomes present in relationships of ethical self-giving, which gives power to those most marginalized in and outside of the community.

The theological differences here affect many other areas that would now fall under philosophy, ethics, anthropology, or natural science, but I especially want to trace the implications for epistemology and political theology. Since, in premodern thinking, knowledge of God was thought to provide the basis for all other knowledge, the idea of divine absence signals a shift in epistemology along with a shift in social power.

If God is absent in the medieval era only as a theoretical limit for human reason, then one can still think of syllogistic logic as the foundation for theology, philosophy, and natural science, as Aquinas does. Nominalist theology, with the help of Luther and other reformers, breaks the continuity of human logic and self-evident knowledge, with the result that one must seek those foundations either in a faithful reading of Scripture (Luther), or an experience of salvation and transformation (Calvin),[25] or, later, in an empirical scientific method or transcendental philosophy (modern science and philosophy).[26]

The major contribution of Anabaptist theology, therefore, is not so much its anti-foundationalism.[27] Indeed, it is more difficult, especially in a postmodern era, to find an example of a "foundationalist" system, at least in the strong sense of the word. But Anabaptist theology does propose a unique epistemology, in which knowledge emerges out of ethical relationships.

The Anabaptist epistemology concerns itself, like other epistemologies, with finding the limits of human knowledge. This starts with the idea of divine absence at the center of the Eucharist. Christ is absent in two senses: first, there is an absence in the elements, which means that the ritual itself does not provide access to the sacred. This implies that knowledge is not attainable by reference to a hierarchical structure of authority, and also that it is not enough to have an individual, internal encounter with the Eucharist. But Christ is also absent in the sense that the ritual is not effective unless there is an accompanying commitment to material acts of solidarity. One gains access to Christ by "sharing body and blood" with one another. So, in epistemological terms, truth is gained only in the crossing of the threshold between self and other. God is mediated to the world in and through material relations.

For many Anabaptists, this has meant an emphasis on consensus in decision-making and biblical interpretation. For example, the early Swiss Anabaptists, who seemed to have developed the most communal form of hermeneutics, described the role of the pastor in an early confession.[28] "The pastor did not preach a binding interpretation of the Scriptures, but instead simply read from them, so that there remained scope for a shared discovery of biblical truth. Interestingly, preaching was not mentioned at all."[29] Thus in comparison with other leadership models in the Reformation, the Anabaptists preferred a "flatter" model in which authority was shared among the community.

The commitment to nonviolence among certain Anabaptist groups flowed naturally from their epistemology. If truth emerges only through relationships, then truth cannot be imposed coercively. Even when some Anabaptists failed to embody the ideals of nonviolence, it continued to function as a measure by which a community could be judged. In Marpeck's 1547 letter to the Swiss Brethren,[30] he confronts them about their scriptural literalism and tendency to excommunicate one another. Marpeck appeals to a shared commitment to nonviolence and links their own intolerance to the persecutions of the Catholics and

Protestants upon the Anabaptists:

> Human coercion will destroy all who [support] a human, forcibly imposed faith and all who claim the Word of faith, but who trust and depend upon human protection and power. . . . Moreover, all the actions, of both the old and new [Catholic and Protestant] forcers of faith, are done in the semblance of Christ and His gospel.[31]

So in the Anabaptist view, nonviolence becomes an important marker of truth. Even if an action is justified by Christian principles, it cannot be considered legitimate if it comes from violence or is maintained by violence.

What the early Anabaptists did not fully consider is that the consensus of a community, perhaps especially a democratic community, can also establish an enclosed identity, a broader "self," in the Levinasian sense. Insofar as everyone within a community has come to agreement, there is no longer a perspective that would require one to "give oneself" in the way that Hubmaier describes. If we extend the Anabaptist logic, then, consensus might actually signify a limit to knowledge, because the other has been forced into the logic of one's own experience, understanding or consciousness. We'll explore this direction more fully in the next two chapters.

Finally, it is important to note that the Anabaptist configuration of divine absence has political implications. To reiterate, the Anabaptist conception of divine absence at the center of the Eucharist displaces "presence" onto the other, the more so the greater the distance between other and self. That placement of divine absence signals not only a shift in epistemology but also a shift in ultimate loyalty or allegiance. If we use Paul Kahn's definition of sovereignty as that which can demand sacrificial violence (see chapter 5), one can see that, in Anabaptism, divine sovereignty reveals itself in the outsider or enemy—not, as is usually the case, in the community itself.

Dirk Willems and the Thiefcatcher

The best practical example of Anabaptist political theology is the story of Dirk Willems, which has become a classic story in Mennonite and Amish communities. Briefly, in 1569 Dirk Willems was being pursued by the authorities, since his adult baptism made him a criminal in the eyes of the state. In the course of pursuit, Willems ran across an ice-covered pond. The heavier thief-catcher who was pursuing Willems fell through the ice and was about to drown. Willems returned to help the man out of the river and saved his life. Despite his kindness, Willems was recaptured and subsequently burnt at the stake.[32] The story was included in *The Martyr's Mirror*, a collection of martyr stories, and the etching by Jan Luyken has become a sort of Mennonite "icon"[33] that captures the spirit of Anabaptist faith.

In terms of political theology, sovereignty appears in this story in the character of the thiefcatcher, because it is this person that presents a demand on Willems' life. To remain faithful, Willems extends himself sacrificially on behalf of this character. Therefore, we get important clues about Anabaptist political theology in the person of the thief-catcher; he represents both a vulnerable individual in need of aid *and* an "enemy," someone from outside the faith community who in fact poses a threat to the community. These two characteristics make the thief-catcher the ideal figure to represent the "sovereign" in the Anabaptist political imagination: if he would not have been vulnerable, Willems would have felt no demand to comply with the thiefcatcher; if he would not have been an enemy, if there had been no existential threat, the story would lose its narrative power as proof of the extent of Willems' faith.

There has been much more ambivalence about the martyr narratives in recent Mennonite writing, and for good reason.[34] Martyr stories can be easily twisted to justify violence. In particular, one has to be careful not to confuse an existential threat that challenges a social identity structure and a simple threat that consists merely in the exercise of power, whether physical or psychological, against a victim. Willems is running away from the simple threat—but is called back by the existential threat. So, if the story of Dirk Willems has lost some of its appeal, it is because the martyr narrative has been used in a sense opposite to the intended meaning. The shift in valuation of the martyr narrative is not due to a weakening of the Mennonite conception of sovereignty but is actually itself an application of that conception.

Here again the connection of divine presence with the outsider or other has important connections to the Anabaptist ethic of nonviolence. Whereas divine sovereignty has usually functioned as a demand on behalf of one's community, which in the modern era is usually the nation-state, the Anabaptist definition of sovereignty locates that existential demand outside of the borders of one's own community. This effectively eliminates the existential need to engage in warfare as a way of safeguarding the sovereign. I explore this aspect of the Anabaptist theology of absence in chapter 5.

The divine absence at the heart of the Gospels became a driving force in the Reformation and, for better or worse, generated a diverse set of competing visions for the church and society. Some of these visions became mainstream and set the stage for the development of the modern world: the Enlightenment, modern science, secular politics, religious toleration. The groups that evolved out of the Radical Reformation mainly existed on the margins of the Western order, partly by choice, and their social influence was modest. Yet the rhythm of absence and presence articulated by Anabaptist theologians is relevant especially in this time when many in the United States feel the poverty of both hyper-nationalist rhetoric and aggressive internationalism exhibited in the 2016 presidential campaign and beyond. Now more than ever, it is important to consider how we might apply the basic insights of the Anabaptist theology of absence to contemporary theology.

THREE

A SPACIOUS PLACE: THEOLOGY THROUGH THE TOMB

"It is God that I can define through human relations and not the inverse. The notion of God—God knows I'm not opposed to it! But when I have to say something about God, it is always beginning from human relations. The inadmissible abstraction is God; it is in terms of the relation with the Other that I speak of God."
—Emmanuel Levinas[1]

When we generalize the insights of the women facing the empty tomb, or Dirk Willems' encounter with the thiefcatcher, we are entering the realm of theology. But the word *theology* can be misleading, especially to modern readers. The root meaning of the word is, of course, "language about God" (*theos* + *logos*), but in an increasingly secular society it becomes difficult to understand what kind of meaningful discourse one could have about God, the common assumption being that one's thoughts about God are a matter of personal faith (or really personal opinion), and that we should keep these thoughts from having any actual impact on the public sphere.

It can also be tempting, even for those who profess a belief in God, to consider theology a less "real" type of discourse than, say, science or sociology. But the issues that traditionally fall within the scope of theology are no less relevant to our world than they were in the medieval era or Reformation, although theological language may need to be translated now. Broader than "God-talk," we should think of theology as a philosophy of the sacred: what is sacred, how does it function, and how is it mediated and maintained? Theology is discourse about ultimate demand, motivation and obligation. It is reflection on the structure of basic values and meaning, which shape the way we situate ourselves toward others and toward the world.

In fact, this is close to the original meaning of the Latin *religio*, from which the English *religion* developed. Religio was not fundamentally about personal devotion to the gods but rather a social obligation. An ancient Roman would say, for example, that making sacrifices at the temple was "religio" for him—an obligation—not only because he believed subjectively in the gods but also because the political and social fabric of the empire was thought to depend on citizens making these sacrifices.[2] The Western division between the public secular sphere and the private religious sphere has masked the continuing relevance to the modern world of "theology" in this broader sense. Many scholars, however, now are uncovering ways the sacred, which used to go by the name "God," appears in different forms in secularism itself.[3]

Theology, then, is an analysis of the sacred, that which makes an ultimate, transcendent demand upon us. And the task of *Christian* theology, I would suggest, is to analyze how the experience of the empty tomb impacts our definition of sacredness, as opposed to other versions of sacredness that we might encounter in daily life.

God and Otherness

To put it in a few words, the empty tomb means that sacredness is without definition in itself. Jesus, the ultimate religious authority and the embodiment of God, is experienced as an absence. As noted in the first chapter, this aspect of the Christian narrative resists the tendency for authority to be solidified and concentrated within a power structure. But at the same time, it produces an enargeic pull—a demand or desire—toward those who are marginalized by current power structures. And when this form of theology is embodied in a community, the result is a demand that presents itself from outside of the communal identity, in direct contradiction to the way that sacredness is usually connected to political identity. The Dirk Willems narrative thus becomes a symbol of the encounter with the absent/present God.

With the Willems story in mind, one could say that when Jesus emerges from the empty tomb, he comes out as a thiefcatcher. There is something about the thiefcatcher that infuses the emptiness of the tomb with theological content. But it is important to be clear about how and why this character can embody the divine in the Anabaptist imagination. If theology is an analysis of sacredness, we can discover the theological meaning of the story by tracing the ultimate demand that lays claim to Willems—the demand that transcends everything else. Certainly that demand does not come from the thiefcatcher's role as a law enforcement officer; at the beginning of the story Willems is unapologetically running away, in flagrant violation of civil law. To give himself up at this point in the story would be merely suicidal, not heroic or faithful. It is only when the thiefcatcher falls through the ice that he appears to embody divine attributes by eliciting a sacrificial act from our protagonist.

In some ways, nothing has changed: Willems and the thiefcatcher are the same people with the same motivations and character traits. Presumably, the thiefcatcher still desires Willems' capture and punishment and Willems has not grown any fonder of the prospect of being burnt at the stake. But there is a sudden power shift between the characters, with the thiefcatcher suddenly becoming vulnerable and Willems in the position to decide whether he lives or dies. The story reveals a corresponding shift in what we might call the realm of the sacred: just when there is a change in power dynamics, there is a shift in the location or concentration of the divine.

The empty tomb has two theological implications: that God cannot be fixed or possessed by any specific figure—and that the *way* that God fluctuates with respect to the material world corresponds inversely to relations of identity and power. So we see in the Willems story that even a thiefcatcher can be a manifestation of God—but only if he is considered under the aspect of vulnerability rather than social power. This means that any theological analysis has to begin with an analysis of relations rather than a description of identity: instead of talking about who or what God is apart from the material world, we look at material relations as an indication of where and how God appears.[4]

In Hubmaier's theology, just as in the empty tomb narratives, God's absence allows for the rediscovery of God in a specific form of community. The self is no longer a container into which divine presence can be poured, or that can have an independent status as saved or damned. Rather, the self emerges through a web of relations upon which forces play and pull to create certain contours. A self is made up of a sort of topological matrix formed by all of its myriad relations. And in general, we can say that God appears to us, from the perspective of a particular topology, in the form of "otherness," as that which has not been or cannot be integrated into our landscape of identity, comfort, or sensibility. God is the inverse space of our topology—a remainder or leftover space.

We sometimes think of "otherness" as synonymous with difference. The "other" is someone who thinks differently than I do, or who looks different, or represents a different culture. But actually we tend to create frameworks that allow us to accommodate difference as part of an intelligible structure, which ends up domesticating or nullifying difference. My friend and I are obviously different people; anyone could name specific physical differences and personality traits that set us apart. It is easy because we have a shared structure that allows us to categorize ourselves as, for instance, brown-eyed, short, extroverted, conscientious—all the characteristics that go into our usual descriptions of people.[5]

These kinds of differences, however, generate no demand upon me because they do not call my self-understanding into question; I can acknowledge these differences without having to rethink anything fundamental. To take a broader social example, we develop racial categories to make sense of phenotypical skin color. The mere fact that there are lighter and darker skin tones might only confirm a pre-established categorization, unless there is some other factor that forces us to think critically about race itself, perhaps a conflict between our self-perception and our relationship to race as a category. It takes an additional "difference" to turn skin color into racism, which actually does generate true otherness.

Therefore, otherness in this technical sense is more than a sum of differences. It is not difference per se that produces otherness but rather a difference that is impossible to perceive or grasp within a given perspective. "This Other is not an opposite, a not-X, but is more appropriately understood as *neither X nor not-X*, as something that does not fall within the 'space' of opposing terms and their intermediaries."[6] And since language works by referring to certain structures of concepts and their oppositions, otherness can never be captured in language. It is always located in a blind spot. Another way of saying it is that power dynamics are a defining feature of our topographical space. Since dominant perspectives are always maintained by some kind of power, the "other" that cannot be contained within this framework is linked to an invisible subaltern space.

The "other" is a manifestation of sovereignty—the one who is absolutely transcendent and therefore makes an ultimate demand upon us.[7] In theological terms, the other is the manifestation of God. We can never fully grasp an encounter with otherness, which is a divine encounter. To understand it or represent it to ourselves, we would have to domesticate it by bringing it under some system of thought, thereby destroying the essence of the experience. But we can, in Deleuze's words, "sense" such an encounter.[8] We might experience otherness as a challenge or a crisis, or perhaps as humility or wonder. If we identify the experience of otherness with the experience of God, we might have a better appreciation for the passages in the Hebrew Bible that emphasize the fear of God and the danger of the divine encounter. The God of Exodus is not a friend, as popular evangelical theology would have us believe. God says, even to Moses, "You cannot see my face and live" (Exod. 33:20). Indeed, if God is defined as the ultimate other, then a full revelation of God would be an unbearable dissolution of the self. We can encounter God only in small doses—the "backside" of God, as it were.

The Woodpecker, My Daughter, and the Sublime

Some time ago, I was walking along a trail in the woods and sat down at a bench overlooking a meadow full of wildflowers. I rested for a while, enjoying the scenery, until I heard a sharp rapping sound. After searching for several minutes, my eye landed on a little woodpecker hopping over a tree branch, pausing now and then to drill for insects. For some reason, it struck me at that moment that this woodpecker had probably been doing this same thing for years and would continue long after I would get up and go home. And next week, when I would be busy with all the responsibilities that had been occupying my thoughts, this woodpecker would be here, pounding away on a tree. In fact it had a complete history that was entirely hidden to me, and an interior life from which I was even more hopelessly excluded. It was a simple thought—one that I am sure many of us have had from time to time—

but it caused a brief, overwhelming shift in the confidence I had of my own place in the world.

This type of feeling is not at all a romantic one, not like what I suspect some people mean when they talk about "finding God in nature." In fact, what was suddenly brought home to me in watching the woodpecker was the utter indifference of the natural world, the great distance between myself and the scene before me, which I had too easily appropriated into a perspective centered on my own enjoyment. It was more like vertigo than gratitude or appreciation. It contained an element of danger, not in the physical but the existential sense. It threatened to undermine my concept of self. This is what Kant calls the "sublime":

> The beautiful in nature is a question of the form of the object, and this consists in limitation, whereas the sublime is to be found in an object even devoid of form, so far as it immediately involves, or else by its presence provokes, a representation of *limitlessness*, yet with a super-added thought of its totality. . . . Moreover, the former delight is very different from the latter in kind. For the beautiful is directly attended with a feeling of the furtherance of life, and is thus compatible with charms and a playful imagination. On the other hand, the feeling of the sublime is a pleasure that only arises indirectly, being brought about by the feeling of a mometary check to the vital forces followed at once by a discharge all the more powerful, and so it is an emotion that seems to be no play, but a serious matter in the exercise of the imagination.[9]

I have felt something similar, only occasionally, when interacting with my children. Here again, the experience of otherness is something very different than the usual portrayal of familial love. For example, it happens sometimes that my five-year-old daughter will do or say something completely unexpected, perhaps just a flash of disdain or skepticism, something that underlines her status as an utterly "other" person with independent agency. Here again, the feeling is a sort of overwhelming uneasiness, or a sudden bursting of one's normal thought process.

In this case, it is not separate from a profound love for my daughter, but it is also not identical to the warm, comforting feeling of connection that I might have when we're playing a game, sharing a memory, or reading a book. In fact, it feels like an interruption of the normal relationship; where "normal" means that I can usually take for granted her responses and actions. The immediate sensation contains both a pull or attraction and a presentiment of danger that comes from recognizing our ultimate independence of each other—a sort of enargeic gap that shows itself in the fabric of family relationships.

These two examples, the woodpecker and my daughter, illustrate the way that otherness can break through even in relationships that seem firmly incorporated into a self-concept. These are exceptional moments that punctuate everyday life and are profound or unsettling but not necessarily unpleasant. Note that otherness is not the result of some objective characteristic, either in the woodpecker or my daughter. Kant argues that the sublime, as something that goes beyond any particular form, cannot be located in an object. Rather, he believes that the source of the sublime is our own mind; we experience the feeling of sublimity (or otherness) when we run up against the limits of our own understanding.[10] It is true that sublimity is not objective, but in his eagerness to reduce everything to the mind, Kant glosses over the fact that these experiences are always the result of an encounter with something. Otherness is always produced by a relation—a specific kind of relation in which our framework for understanding the world is exceeded. And since these frameworks are created and maintained with social power, otherness or sacredness is also a function of social power.

Otherness and Social Power

Therefore, we are most likely to encounter otherness in situations where systemic power relations are unveiled, and these encounters are often more persistent and painful than the previous examples. They are experiences that reveal the inadequacy of our previous thinking to cope with reality. For a middle-class person, this might take the form of walking past a homeless man sitting on the sidewalk with a cardboard sign. Donald Trump's election in 2016 might have produced a similar feeling among liberal white voters, as well as the events in Charlottesville, Virginia the following summer, in that both events punctured the comfortable idea that the United States is progressing toward an inclusive, post-racial reality.

At the college where I work, we try to encourage this unsettling type of experience by requiring North American students to study and do service assignments in international settings, particularly in the

Global South. The goal is to encourage experiences that puncture one's self-image and challenge the definitions that we have used to divide the world into manageable categories. They reveal some kind of responsibility that could have been ignored previously (whether or not aware of it intellectually) but now has to be taken into account.

There is no guarantee that we will react constructively to these encounters; more often we try to escape as soon as possible back to our previous ways of perceiving. Still, the experience of otherness tends to operate on us unconsciously even when we try to repress it.

And what is this demand that otherness makes upon us? As Emmanuel Levinas says, the demand of the other is both infinite and content-less but at the same time concrete and personal. My encounter with the woodpecker struck me not because I understood something new about birds or nature in general, or even about woodpeckers, but rather because I saw *this* bird as a real individual with a life independent of me and valuable apart from my own valuation. But the encounter did not necessarily reveal a particular response that I should make. If there were a system of ethics that we could appeal to to know how to respond to an encounter with otherness, we would have already domesticated that encounter to fit inside a system.[11]

One might say that the other at least demands recognition, respect, dignity or nonviolence; according to Levinas the primal demand is simply: "thou shalt not commit murder." But beyond this, an ethical response cannot be determined ahead of time. It has to emerge out of our encounter with the other. Rather than appealing to a higher authority, we have to begin with a kind of emptiness, with a desire for something that is not already present and also not previously imagined. The demand of the other is more like a question than a command—What will you do? or Who will you decide to be?—but it is a question that must be answered in one way or another.

The desire or demand that otherness generates is paradoxical because it points toward its own domestication or even destruction in its very appeal for recognition. We cannot simply dwell in the pure experience of otherness. We are called to draw some kind of conclusion, or make some ethical claim, or take some action. I come out of my experience in the woods with a renewed commitment to preserving public green spaces, or I am reminded of my responsibility to provide a positive and healthy future for my daughter.

In each of these cases, by generalizing the experience or adjusting my personal worldview, I have in fact attempted to make that otherness a part of myself. Humanitarian work is an attempt to domesticate suffering into a system of aid that can be managed and understood and even used to build up a sense of self. To the extent that I make a successful response to the other, I bring the other into myself and am no longer challenged by it. The full domestication of some concrete other may take some time, even a lifetime, but the basic movement is the same in each case.

This domestication is always a dangerous project, because it involves reducing the other to an element in some system. We can and do fail when we come face to face with the other. Therefore domestication always requires re-encounters with otherness that will destabilize whatever response has been made previously. The primal experience of the empty tomb is followed by attempts to make that experience concrete in the early church, and eventually more institutionalized forms of Christianity, but the empty tomb as the primal grammar of Christianity continues to inject a certain restlessness, sometimes even unruliness or fragility, into Christian communities (as we see particularly in and after the Reformation). It is that same grammar that has to infuse Christian responses to God and others.

What we experience as otherness or sacredness depends on the position or perspective that we occupy. The way we view the world determines the extent to which an event will challenge us or simply confirm what we have already taken into account. But otherness is not a simple matter of personal choice; our sense of self is based on communal, social and political structures that encourage automatic and largely unconscious assumptions. Insofar as these structures apply broadly across a whole population, one can make public, objective claims about God. So, for instance, given the history of race in the United States, and the fact that American racial categories have been exported all over the world, one can now say quite literally that "God is black."[12]

The Self as Landscape

The unique blend of social-political and personal perspective that we occupy is what constitutes our "self." But that means that our "selves" are never a matter of simple identities—not things that are contained or possessed. Rather, we are who we are because we each survey a particular landscape, corresponding to our relations with the material world, but with its contours defined and distorted by centers of power. One could draw an analogy with the way that a planet's gravity distorts the fabric of space-time. Our perceptions are alternatively heightened or diminished depending on the shape of our landscape. The legal system that we inhabit, for instance, shapes a landscape in which some injustices can be expressed and others remain invisible. The structure of Western land rights allowed colonizers to take land from indigenous peoples and gain legal rights. There is no possibility of legal recourse in this case because earlier indigenous land use did not fall into the sort of categories recognized in the legal system (i.e., the concept of "land rights" itself is a foreign one).

Marx recognized that the power of capital creates certain blind spots in our economic landscape, so that the relation between worker and capitalist appears to both parties to be equitable and normal.[13] Gilles Deleuze gives the example of Michel Foucault's work with the prison system in France:

> Foucault's establishment of the Prison Information Group . . . came from the fact that 'what he saw was actually intolerable. . . .' It was intolerable, not because it was unjust, but because no one saw it, because it was imperceptible. But everyone knew it. It was no secret. Everyone knew about this prison in the prison, but no one saw it. Foucault *saw* it.[14]

These multiple lines of power—legal, economic, political, and more—interact as they converge on a single event. All make their contribution to one's perceptual landscape, just as a combination of natural forces shape a physical landscape in often dramatic and unpredictable ways.

If the self is a landscape, otherness (and therefore God) is the parallel, opposite space above or within that landscape, something like a photographic negative of our perception. We experience the sacred as an intensification of space, an imposition of all that interstitial stuff that fills up the cracks between whatever objects have been coalescing out of our thinking. God is that which hovers above the topology of the self-landscape, generating mirages that call our very senses into question. Just as our physical sight is naturally attracted to the objects in our field of vision, our self-perspective offers up objects that dominate our consciousness. But to encounter God we have to attend to the ambiguity that plays around the "objects" of our perspective.

Since a self is always constituted by a collection of relationships, there is no simple identification of self and otherness with an individual person. A person is never just a "self" or just an "other." It is possible to be alienated from certain aspects of one's own identity—for example, when power systems make it impossible to express something about oneself. There can be a "double consciousness" that results from having to live a subaltern identity within a dominant system. It forces an individual in a sense to hold together conflicting horizons in a single landscape. In that case, otherness may be experienced as something internal; God is with us. An encounter with otherness in this form can produce what liberation theologians call "epistemological privilege," the ability to see God more completely than others. According to Bonino, the poor are able

> to see and understand what the rich and powerful cannot see nor understand. It is not that their sight is perfect, it is the place where they are which makes the difference. Power and richness have a distortionary effect—they freeze our view of reality. The point of view of the poor, on the other hand, pierced by suffering and attracted by hope, allows them, in their struggles, to conceive another reality.[15]

But here again one needs caution, because it is easy to mistake epistemological privilege for its opposite—a reaction of the self against the discomfort that otherness produces. How does one tell the difference, for example, between the status of racism and "reverse racism"? Here especially, theology depends on an honest analysis of social power. Even when whiteness is technically a minority, it is not an existential minority and therefore not a vehicle for otherness. As Deleuze says,

> The opposition between minority and majority is not simply quantitative. Majority implies a constant, of expression or content, serving as a standard measure by which to evaluate it. Let us suppose that the constant or standard is the average adult-white-heterosexual-European-male speaking a standard language. . . . It is obvious that "man" holds the majority, even if he is less numerous than mosquitoes, children, women, blacks, peasants, homo-

sexuals, etc. That is because he appears twice, once in the constant and again in the variable from which the constant is extracted.[16]

Contrary to orthodox theology, God is not omnipresent. In fact, because we necessarily see things through dominant systems (and even when we try to see in a non-dominant way, we only succeed by constructing a different system), it would be more accurate to call God omni-absent. The divine space is always receding from us, always on the horizon and topographically indeterminate. We only occupy the space that God has vacated before us. But this space nonetheless generates a dynamism or flow, which drives the self as a modulating series of events rather than a substantial subject or object.

Therefore, just as we need to transition to a relational theology to make sense of the absent Christ, we also need to transition to a process-based metaphysics that makes events rather than substances the primary basis of reality. The next chapter engages this task.

FOUR

UN/GODLY FLOODS: METAPHYSICS AFTER THE TOMB

"The action of the fourth phase is the love of God for the world. . . . What is done in the world is transformed into a reality in heaven, and the reality in heaven passes back into the world. By reason of this reciprocal relation, the love in the world passes into the love in heaven, and floods back again into the world. In this sense, God is the great companion—the fellow-sufferer who understands."
—Alfred North Whitehead[1]

Metaphysics is even less possible today than theology. Partly this is due to the triumph of nominalism and its allergy to rationalist, *a priori* systems.[2] Luther and other Protestants believed scholastic metaphysics to be a usurpation of the divine authority that properly resided either in Scripture or the individual. The more radical Anabaptists were even less likely to subscribe to abstract intricacies produced by the academic and ecclesial elite.[3] And since Western secularism is a byproduct of Protestant nominalism, metaphysics as a discipline has been ignored by scientists and philosophers alike.

There are, after all, good reasons to be suspicious of metaphysics. As early as the sixteenth century, the Anabaptists had intuited the link between formal, systematic thought and violence, largely due to their position as an outlawed and persecuted religious group in sixteenth-century Europe. Even if they would not have articulated these insights in the same form, early Anabaptists might have agreed with Derrida or Foucault that metaphysics or metanarratives tend to both uphold and mask systems of domination.

At the same time, there are other forms of violence that can remain even in nonfoundational systems, and these have been more difficult for Anabaptists as well as postmodern philosophers to overcome. Narratives, for instance, can contain a wide variety of violent themes, and are particularly adept at hiding this violence from those who subscribe to their underlying symbolic systems.[4]

For example, the Anabaptist narrative of martyrdom, which originally functioned as an anti-authority symbol, tended later on to obscure the way that Mennonite settlers benefited from colonialism in the United States, or participated in class stratification in pre-Communist Russia. Elaine Enns has traced Mennonites' involvement in the displacement of indigenous people in both Eastern Europe and North America, all in the name of religious freedom and nonviolence.[5] Similarly, the narrative of God's eschatological violence has subtly encouraged political quietism or environmental destruction, even when it is linked to the present nonviolence of the church.[6] Narratives themselves have to be constantly interrogated if we do not wish to perpetuate violence, but this interrogation cannot be done within the logic of the narrative.

This is where the systematicness usually associated with metaphysics can play an important role. In its demand for comprehensiveness and coherence, metaphysics requires us to seek out counternarratives in an attempt to reconcile them with our own assumptions. In the process, our own views may have to be modified or abandoned. We cannot rest in the narrative that we inherit about our origins or place in the world, especially when we encounter other stories that do not fit with existing interpretations. The difficulty is that the very drive toward comprehensiveness contains the drive toward violence. If we expect to be able to integrate all narratives into a single universal truth, we will always end up imposing a self-serving truth and brushing aside inconvenient anomalies.

Micrometaphysics of the Empty Tomb

The empty tomb serves the purpose of a self-interrogating system in Christian thought (not a narrative per se, but always, at least potentially, an anti-narrative). It is at the same time a historical-material anchor and the origin of a cosmology. The event itself is incomprehensible apart from the material context of first-century Palestine, so it has an unavoidably local character. And the logic of the empty tomb also, as we have seen, points the reader back to whatever "Galilee" they find themselves in (i.e., whatever perspectival landscape they inhabit). But at the same time, the empty tomb produces the cosmic Christ of Colossians or John. One of the earliest Christian confessions was "Jesus is Lord." We find in the tomb a pattern that holds good for the entire universe. Here historicity and universality are actually co-constitutive, not antagonistic.[7] Instead of a single universal system, the result is "universalities," systems that originate in particular contexts but interpret all of reality. The gospels are an example of a set of universalities: each are based in specific, material events, and each produces a very different world which can be extended and exported to interpret other contexts.

In a way, this form of metaphysics mirrors the recent turn toward microhistory, in which history is narrated through the lens of a particular event, community, or object rather than pretending to an objective viewpoint.[8] Though microhistorians often focus on a very specific event, their goal is to illuminate larger historical questions and to pay attention to the way that the particular event relates to its broader context.[9] In the process, one is able to uncover a very different picture of history:

> [I]f one wishes to rescue the unknown from oblivion, a new conceptual and methodological approach to history is called for that sees history no longer as a unified process, a grand narrative in which the many individuals are submerged, but as a multifaceted flow with many individual centers.[10]

Rather than emphasizing broad movements of history to encompass people in general, microhistorians look for the outliers of history—individuals or communities that deviate from the norm, and thereby emphasize the diversity and conflict within history.[11]

We might similarly call a metaphysics of the empty tomb a kind of "micrometaphysics."[12] Micrometaphysics differs from traditional metaphysics in that it seeks out and highlights discrepancies between systems, especially departures from dominant metaphysical assumptions. The micrometaphysics of a given community may or may not converge with those of other communities, but each metaphysical system does seek to make claims that go beyond the boundaries of the community and may be relevant for others. We can learn from the metaphysics of communities other than our own; in fact, we should expect to be able to learn things that would have been impossible to understand given our own particular circumstances. Since micrometaphysics works at a concrete, local level, we should expect a multiplicity of metaphysical systems that interact with one another as they emerge from the unique interpretations of individuals and communities.[13] Constructing metaphysics in this way is to respect particularity as an ultimate fact, not something to be overcome, even eschatologically, in universality.[14] But it does suggest that each particularity is an interpretation of *all* of experience, and is therefore universal in scope.

In previous chapters, we have seen how the encounter at the empty tomb is experienced as an erotic spaciousness which pulls us toward material "others." Thus, we already have an idea of God and the self: the self as a network of relations shaped by various social forces and God as the always-receding space in which this network develops. But the empty tomb, like all symbols, functions not only on the psychological or subjective level, but cosmologically as well. What we think about ourselves is inseparable from what we think about the world. Specifically, the metaphysical "grammar" of the empty tomb sets up a relational rather than substance-based metaphysics. The self is not a fixed or finite entity that exists independently and apart from its environment; therefore neither is its environment made up of separate, independent entities. It is more appropriate to think in terms of events or flows than substances.

Whitehead's Metaphysical Contribution

We might make use here of the metaphysics developed by the mathematician and philosopher Alfred North Whitehead. He defines both the world and God in terms of a creative emergence of related events. God functions as the lure toward novel, complex experience, and the world, in its process of decision, actualizes and differentiates God. Each is mutually immanent in the other, and each transcends the other in some way. Though Whitehead conceived of God as the repository of an unchanging network of potentials ("eternal objects"), many process theologians have modified this view.

For Anabaptists, perhaps the most significant shift in process theology has been toward a God that functions as an elicitor of value rather than a conservator of value. This idea of God has significant overlap with Anabaptist ecclesiology—particularly, but not exclusively, John Howard Yoder's ecclesiology, though it would make certain corrections to Yoder (see below). Doing Anabaptist metaphysics through a process lens would allow for an articulation of the God/world relationship in which God provides space for the world to construct value through communal and ecological relationships.

As noted above, the building blocks of Whitehead's universe are not atomic objects, as in Newtonian physics, but "drops of experience," which he called "actual events," "actual entities," or "actual occasions."[15] Each event emerges out of the influences of the past, creates its own unique configuration of these influences, and then contributes its decision to future events. This means that in each event that occurs, the past limits the range of possibilities open to subsequent events, but does not determine the future. Consciousness as we know it is a phenomenon that emerges only in more developed organisms, but there is a "subjective" side to every event in which potential possibilities collapse into a definite state. Whitehead separates the causal and the subjective factors of each event into "physical and mental poles." The physical pole of the event refers to influences received from the past within a space of potential that is God. The mental pole refers to the subjective decision of the event as it becomes determinate.

It was important to Whitehead *not* to introduce God into his metaphysics as a *deus ex machina*.[16] "In the first place, God is not to be treated as an exception to all metaphysical principles, invoked to save their collapse. He is their chief exemplification." Whitehead was frustrated by previous attempts to "save" metaphysical systems by reference to a transcendent source of order. Not only is the idea of a being who imposes a metaphysical scheme from without intellectually unsatisfying, Whitehead believed, but it also contributes to the violence of the monotheistic traditions.

> [T]he doctrine of an aboriginal, eminently real, transcendent creator, at whose fiat the world came into being, and whose imposed will it obeys, is a fallacy which has infused tragedy into

the histories of Christianity and of Mahometanism [sic].

When the Western world accepted Christianity, Caesar conquered; and the received text of Western theology was edited by his lawyers.... The brief Galilean vision of humility flickered throughout the ages, uncertainly.... But the deeper idolatry, of the fashioning of God in the image of the Egyptian, Persian, and Roman imperial rulers, was retained. The Church gave unto God the attributes which belonged exclusively to Caesar.[17]

So Whitehead must begin with different assumptions than those of previous theologians. For one, God must be considered as a part of the metaphysical system, which, for Whitehead, meant thinking about God as an actual entity. This has significant theological implications. Like any other entity, God has both a physical and mental pole. In God, the mental pole represents the infinite, eternal realm of eternal objects or possibilities—the primordial nature of God. Because Whitehead believed, like Plato, that the appearance of abstractions in the world necessitated some metaphysical realm of abstractions, he conceived of the primordial nature as the set of all possible potentials. These potentials are then available for actual entities as they move from the ambiguity of the past to a definite decision. This also makes God the "principle of concretion," the one who provides for the possibility of definiteness in lieu of complete ambiguity or chaos.[18] In the primordial nature, God is considered impersonally, as the ground of reality and experience.

On the other hand, the physical pole is God's conscious experience of the world. Just as other actual entities receive the entirety of past decisions into their own subjective life, God receives the entirety of the world's decisions. There are, of course, several key differences between God and the world, the most important being that God's mental pole is infinite and therefore singular, whereas the mental poles of other actual entities are limited to their own historical perspective:

A physical pole is in its own nature exclusive, bounded by contradiction: a conceptual pole is in its own nature all-embracing, unbounded by contradiction. The former derives its share of infinity from the infinity of appetition; the latter derives its share of limitation from the exclusiveness of enjoyment. Thus, by reason of [God's] priority of appetition, there can be but one primordial nature for God; and, by reason of their priority of enjoyment, there must be one history of many actualities in the physical world.[19]

In other words, the movement of God and the world mirror each other—God moves from unity to multiplicity, and the world moves from multiplicity to unity.[20]

The interaction of the dipolar entities of the world and the dipolar God yield a cyclic process of co-creation. The temporal world is

> perfected by its reception and its reformation, as a fulfillment of the primordial appetition which is the basis of all order. In this way God is completed by the individual, fluent satisfactions of finite fact, and the temporal occasions are completed by their everlasting union with their transformed selves.[21]

For the sake of simplicity, Whitehead summarizes his system as a cycle with four phases: the primordial vision of God which includes all possible futures, the multiplicity of the world which arises from this ground of possibility, the harmony of this multiplicity in God's experience of the world, and the world's reception of God's understanding.[22] God is immanent in the world by virtue of the order and lure that God provides; the world is immanent in God as it is taken up into God's consequent nature. Both transcend each other in their novel synthesis of experience.

In Whitehead's metaphysics, one of the basic principles is that causation must be grounded in reality. Whitehead calls this the "ontological principle:" every occurrence must have its origin or cause in another real occasion.[23] However, Whitehead also wants to affirm the possibility of radical novelty, or novelty that does not arise from one's past. This seems to contradict the ontological principle because this kind of novelty would appear to arise out of nothing. Whitehead solves this dilemma by positing a realm of pure potentials, the "eternal objects," that exist within the primordial nature of God.[24] God orders these eternal objects and offers them to each unfolding event as part of the "initial aim" or purpose for the event. God is therefore the source of novelty and the appraiser of the value of future possibilities.[25] This makes possible a lure toward certain possibilities over others, which is experienced by the occasion as a kind of conscience or pull toward the good.

The Disappearance of the Eternal Objects

However, this quasi-Platonic aspect of Whitehead's philosophy has been less and less attractive to later process theologians. For example, Lewis Ford makes a major modification to process theology by defining God as future creativity. In particular, Ford's theology differs from earlier versions of process theology in that God is no longer the repository of eternal objects. This poses a problem for Ford because the initial aim is traditionally mediated by eternal objects. He describes the dilemma: "As noted [in Ford's modification], eternal objects cannot characterize creativity, and hence cannot be used for the infusion of aim. On the other hand, if future creativity were to lack all form, it could not affect the present at all."[26] Ford suggests that God affects the world by means of "subjective forms," which are less concrete than the objectifiable eternal objects. "An aim shapes creativity, but it cannot be abstracted from its creativity to be objectified. Objectification requires a certain definite being that is to be objectified, and this creativity lacks, even if informed by aim."[27] The subjective forms provide some features to future creativity, which allow for its pluralization and infusion into the present, but remain indefinite.

Despite the vagueness of the subjective form, however, Ford agrees with Whitehead and John Cobb that the aim is characterized by a divine valuation of potential outcomes. "At the outset the aim is that value most appropriate to the particular world of actualities existing for that occasion."[28] The difference is that Ford defines this aim more contextually. Ford notes that "because he regarded eternal objects to be uncreated," Whitehead, "could only admit definite forms. Hence, the initial subjective aim was taken to be definite, derived from a nontemporal definite valuation, independent of the temporal course of events." On the contrary, Ford proposes that God's valuation of potential must be "firmly rooted in the temporal process of actualization of a given locus."[29] In other words, God's valuation of the future cannot be forever fixed, but becomes increasingly defined as the present makes its advance into the future.

Catherine Keller moves even further toward an indefinite God, abandoning any concrete initial aim at all. Keller suggests that God's goodness might be more open-ended than process theologians have previously thought. "Rather," Keller says,

I am trying to think a complex goodness . . . which is not in fact offering a positive lure for every occasion. Or for any occasion. The specific lure, as the initial aim of every occasion, need not be understood as encoded with a particular, father-knows-best . . . sort of content.[30]

Instead, Keller proposes an aim that is better characterized as the ground of an occasion's well-being. God does not privilege a particular outcome as God's unambiguous "will," but rather gives hints of possibilities that must be discovered by the occasion itself.

By abandoning the idea of God as the orderer and presenter of specific potentials for the world, Keller moves toward a God that is manifested to us as absence or capacity. That is, God becomes the space into which the world ventures. "A 'capacity' signifies—unlike a mere act or force—an ability to receive, and so to give *place* (as a room has a seating 'capacity'). . . . Theologically this means: it is then not that the world is simply *capax dei* . . . but that God is *capax mundi*."[31] Yet Keller wants to retain the "principle of limitation" by which God might suggest some possibilities over others, a sort of "divine wisdom," although this would not be as prescriptive as Whitehead or even Ford believe. She identifies this capacity of God with the traditional concept of the "Godhead" or Whiteheadian "creativity," and the divine differentiation that occurs within this capacity with such terms as Elohim, Sophia, Logos and Christ.[32]

How can this differentiation be reconciled with the infinite capacity, space, or absence of God? This question is essential if our metaphysics of the empty tomb is to allow both for creative freedom and for a God who looks on the world with real concern. It is a delicate point—if differentiation is conceived of in too specific of terms, then God collapses into the paternal arranger of things; if the capacity of God is left without any ability to differentiate, then God becomes an impersonal force that does not care which possibilities are actualized in the world.

Keller suggests a third space that helps mediate between the transcendent and the incarnational—the *ruach* or Spirit. "Apart from the spirit 'brooding o'er the chaos,' Tehom [the "deep"] remains a sterile possibility and 'God' remains mere Word, fleshless abstraction and power code. Only through pneumatology does theology have a prayer."[33] As in Augustine, Spirit signifies relationship itself, but Keller broadens the scope of Spirit beyond the divine relationship of Father and Son to include the interrelations of the world.[34] The Spirit is characterized by the practice of love in conditions of difference, by a "collective process of infinite reciprocations and devastating sensitivities."[35] In Spirit, the world becomes the body of the incarnated Logos. In other words, the differentiation of God is accomplished through a worldly process of love amid otherness and conflict.

Bringing together Keller's pneumatology and Ford's conception of the divine as future, we come to a metaphysics in which the present world is always being called forth into the waiting space of God. Rather than presenting any particular possibility or set of possibilities, or even any particular "subjective form," God mediates and elicits a response from one event to the rest of creation. God pulls the world forward into a future that must wait to be shaped by its own decisions. Insofar as the events in the world respond to God with reciprocation, sensitivity and love, God is differentiated and contextualized—in short, "incarnated"—in the world.

An Argument for Heterodoxy

To many Christians, including Mennonites and other Anabaptists, the theology and metaphysics stated above might seem more like a threat than a resource. Some would argue that "Anabaptist theology" should be seen as a species of orthodox Christian Protestantism, if indeed one can even define Anabaptist theology as distinct from Christianity in general.[36] To these theologians, the perennial tendency of Anabaptists to downplay or revise classical theological statements causes a great deal of anxiety. Reimer acknowledges that "historicism" (emphasis on ethics, politics, and community rather than creeds) is a direct consequence of the "modernizing" spirit of early Anabaptism, but he sees this as a very dangerous habit.[37] Others have tried to redeem the early Anabaptists as basically orthodox, usually citing the fact that Anabaptists drew on patristic sources or trinitarian language for their theology.[38]

However, if one interprets Anabaptism as merely a subset of orthodox theology, process philosophy is hardly relevant to the task of constructing an Anabaptist metaphysics. In fact, it would only be necessary to weave certain Anabaptist distinctives (nonviolence, Christocentrism, etc.) into the classical creedal statements to achieve a better balance between historical and metaphysical themes.[39]

The root of the tension between Anabaptism and orthodoxy, and the reason that scholars have had such difficulty reconciling the two, lies in a fundamental disagreement about the sources of theological knowledge. For Anabaptists, theological interpretation is only legitimate as a lived, communal endeavor. Classical theologians consider the basic Christian claims to be timeless and unalterable, though of course they may also be subject to some interpretation.

The problem is not just that the creeds were developed amid the "Constantinian shift" as a way to bypass the ethics of the Gospels. The tension would have remained if, for instance, the earliest Christian communities had attempted to create creeds of their own that would be binding on all future Christians. The question is, how much agency does any particular Christian community have in its hermeneutic role over against ecclesial and academic authorities? If one believes that the community plays a non-trivial role in the production of theological knowledge, and that this knowledge is always necessarily a response to the context of that community, then one cannot affirm orthodox theological claims *a priori*. Insofar as the creeds help to make sense of a particular context, they may play an important role (indeed they were crucial ways of answering theological questions that came up in fourth-century Europe), but their relevance to contemporary questions would have to be discerned case by case.

To engage in an Anabaptist micrometaphysics would be to say that the way we have experienced God at work in the Christian community (and not community in general but in this particular historical, cultural tradition) reveals the way that God works with the world. There would obviously be various ways of articulating the idea of co-creation or of God's immanence in the faith community, yet the categories of process thought hold great potential to enrich Anabaptist metaphysics.

Probably the most important addition of process theology to this discussion is the idea that the world contributes something essential to the life of God. It is only through the actions of the world that God is differentiated and actualized, and, at least for many process theologians, the world actually plays a significant role in constructing or discovering value. It is necessary from an Anabaptist perspective to think of God as eliciting value from the world rather than imposing it or even possessing it as a pre-given system of possibilities. Otherwise the work of the church is irrelevant; it is a mere imitation of a heavenly reality, and its interpretations play no role in shaping God's vision for the future.

The Anabaptist God, like the process God, is based on the fragile "Galilean vision of humility." God does not impose an order on the world but provides the impulse toward creative, relational community. God creates by calling forth a plurality of interrelated moments, and urging us to somehow make out of this multiplicity an aesthetic, complex composition. Though the language of primordial and consequent natures may seem foreign, God works in a twofold way: as a lure or a capacity that provides the impulse for the world to create (primordial nature), and as a host who allows space for this creative work and sympathetically evaluates the result (consequent nature).

God is not simply present to the world; if one is searching for transcendent value or meaning, all that one encounters is a space, an absence. From the perspective of the present, God is always withdrawing into the future to make more space for the creative movement of the world. From an Anabaptist perspective, however, this withdrawal allows us to find God again as we engage others in our community, our neighbors, and, perhaps especially, our enemies. The Spirit of God is present in all the reciprocations and sensitivities of the world, encouraging and authorizing creative love wherever it appears.[40]

Process theology also suggests a way for Anabaptists to reclaim the transcendence of God, not, as Reimer would suggest, by abandoning the criticism of foundationalism and orthodoxy, but by emphasizing God's constant lure toward greater aesthetic achievement. If God functions as an impulse to move beyond current structures and worldviews, then God is "radically free from our systems of morality and our vision of what God ought to be."[41] But the transcendence of God does not point toward an unknowability between violence and nonviolence. It points toward "nonviolences" that are beyond our limited imaginations. God appears always in those who are marginalized or who do not fit within current social structures.

The idea of transcendence in the process framework is important because it helps guard against possible abuses of communitarian ethics. John Howard Yoder's sexual violence against women students and acquaintances is a good example of this potential pitfall. Yoder had a very optimistic view of what the community can achieve in its hermeneutical process. He assumed that if everyone is given the chance to speak, the community will arrive at a conception of justice or ethics that more or less reflects God's will for the community (though this must always be held lightly and humbly). For Yoder, God is most often identified with what is voiced within the community.

This neglects the power relationships that are already present in the structure of a communal decision.[42] The terms of discourse tend to privilege certain voices and silence others. As Lyotard says, we need to pay more attention to what cannot be voiced in a particular framework rather than the consensus that occurs within that framework.[43] Yoder's lack of awareness of power differences within the community and of his own responsibility as a leading scholar allowed him to dismiss the concerns of his victims because they could not be voiced within the dominant systems of administration and church politics.

The transcendence of God is related to the idea of divine judgment, although this too must be interpreted carefully. If God does not in fact provide an occasion with a specific aim, there will be no specific standard from which God might judge it apart from the content that flows into God from the events of the world. In other words, the divine standard depends on, or follows along the lines of, the interactions of events, just as a horizon depends on the contours of a physical landscape. But in the context of a specific relationship or conflict, God uncovers the extent to which an occasion succeeds in its response to the divine call toward creative reconciliation. In our relationships with others in the world, then, we mutually construct for one another our judgment as well as our salvation. The interpretation of Matthew 18:18, "whatever you bind on earth will be bound in heaven, and whatever you loose on earth will be loosed in heaven," is not that we (individually or communally) can define ethics arbitrarily but that ethics follows lines of power that flow between events.

This may appear to be a "soft" kind of judgment, one that waters down the divine prerogative to define and erase evil from creation. Reimer would worry that the transfer of eschatological power from God to the world makes impossible any hope for future justice. Yet the view of judgment offered by this theology is no less demanding or "secure" than orthodox views, although it is always relative, ongoing, and open-ended. In fact, because everything in the cosmos exists in relationship, God's judgment would always be infinite, in that it incorporates our accountability to every other event that we encounter. Although God will not impose justice onto the future, God is always working in and with the concrete decisions of the world, not only toward justice but toward greater and more complete understandings of the meaning of justice.

Brief Summary

To summarize the material so far—the biblical narrative, the historical Anabaptist theology, the theological and metaphysical generalizations—we might finally articulate a set of metaphysical principles that attempt to capture the emptiness that is at the root of Christian experience. We have first the emptiness itself, corresponding to the tomb discovered on the first Easter morning. The tomb-space signifies not only the absence of Christ but Christ *as* absence. In other words, this is a space that is without content but nonetheless laden with authority and potential. It generates but does not prescribe the particularities that precipitate out of it.

What emerges within the divine absence is a relation. Since a relation is two-dimensional, one might describe it in geometrical terms as a line. But since a relation is also asymmetrical and incorporates a power differential, it would be better to think of it as a vector—a line that contains information about location, direction, and force. A vector is always concrete and unique and cannot be abstracted from its actual setting.

A confluence of vectors could be called an event, as Whitehead does, and this terminology has the advantage of highlighting flow and impermanence. However, it also is misleading in that it implies something self-contained and bounded. Rather, we should think in terms of networks or topographies: collections of vectors that create specific shapes, just as a set of lines can be arranged to create a curve, or in the same way that a landscape can be defined in terms of horizons and distances. Only at this level do we find subjects and objects. A self, and any other object for that matter, is in fact a collection of relations, and its "shape" or contextual situatedness, depends on the particular relations that have defined it. Substances are therefore preceded and constituted by their relations rather than vice versa.

With these metaphysical principles in mind, in the following chapters we can now test some applications in three areas: political theology, ecological theology, and nonviolent ethics.

FIVE

CHAPTER 5

THE KING AND THE ENEMY: TRACES OF SOVEREIGNTY

So when recruits have been carefully selected who excel in mind and body, and after daily training for four or more months, a legion is formed by order and auspices of the invincible Emperor. The soldiers are marked with tattoos in the skin which will last and swear an oath, when they are enlisted on the rolls. That is why (the oaths) are called the "sacraments" of military service. . . . For since the Emperor has received the name of the "August," faithful devotion should be given, unceasing homage paid him as if to a present and corporeal deity. For it is God whom a private citizen or a soldier serves, when he faithfully loves him who reigns by God's authority. The soldiers swear that they will strenuously do all that the Emperor may command, will never desert the service, nor refuse to die for the Roman State.
—Vegetius, fourth century CE[1]

Just as in the Reformation, the mediation of the sacred to the community is key to understanding the relationship of citizens to the modern state. Whereas ultimate sovereignty used to be reserved for God (although in practice it was mediated through the church), those divine attributes were transferred around the time of the Reformation onto the monarch of a nation-state and then, in the American and French revolutions, onto the general population as "popular sovereignty." And so even in modern democracies, the nation still plays the same divine role. It can demand from its citizens that they sacrifice their own lives in defense of the nation; it gives and enforces the law, even as it exists itself above the law; and it creates a system of cultural or religious practices and rituals to maintain its authority.

The sacramental theology outlined in the previous two chapters argues for a very different configuration of sacredness and political identity. The difference that the absent Christ makes to this discussion is clearest when compared to other contemporary political theologies. Here, we consider two theorists who are specifically concerned with the relationship of religion and violence in the modern state: René Girard, the French philosopher and anthropologist, and Paul Kahn, professor of constitutional law at Yale University.

Sacrifice, Religion, and Violence

The analysis of religion and violence has often been framed by the notion of sacrifice. Violence comes in the form of sacrifice, either of another or oneself, to whatever is considered sacred. The sacred, which represents ultimate meaning or loyalty, is allowed to manifest itself through violence only because the idea of sacrifice demands that we defend these loyalties at any cost. This may occur either through a scapegoat, as in René Girard, or through the operation of the sovereign, as in Paul Kahn's work. Both these authors recognize that so-called "secular" loyalties of Western citizenship function as the contemporary form of the sacred, which only serves to broaden the relevance of the sacrificial model.[2] If indeed many forms of violence in our world are products of systems of sacrifice, it becomes important to understand the religious motivations behind violence, even when this violence masquerades simply as national maintenance.

In Western political theology, Christ has been one of the key symbols in the attempt to understand, criticize, and transcend the violence of sacrifice. Girard, for instance, believes that the Gospels have permanently disclosed the scapegoat mechanism that relieves societies from the pressure of mimetic violence, although this disclosure has mostly been ignored by a nominally Christian society. Kahn suggests that Christ undermines the idea of sovereignty (and therefore sacrifice) by his universality, although our political systems remain mired in their own particularity. In either case, Christ functions as the potential, but unrealized, possibility of transcending the sacredness that ultimately causes violence. As in Barth, Christianity is in some way the religion-less religion[3] and therefore marks a way beyond violence.

The empty tomb offers a different model for the relationship between Christ, sovereignty, and sacrifice. Rather than separating Christ from sovereignty or sacredness, as Girard and Kahn do, we should recognize Christ as representing a form of sovereignty that is the negative correlate of political sovereignty. In a political sense, the sovereign is the locus of collective power and identity. The sovereign represents the community and demands total and exclusive loyalty from that community.

On the other hand, in Christ, sovereignty is dissolved into whatever lies external to the communal identity. Christ is not the simple absence or abolishment of sovereignty; Christ ends sacrificial violence by demanding loyalty on behalf of those outside the community. Christ is a sovereign that has no location or identity—the non/sovereign—which is not the same as *not* being a sovereign.

Girard's Proposal

Girard's work is probably the most important route by which the sacrificial nature of violence has been analyzed. According to Girard, the mimetic nature of human desire means that communities always inevitably find themselves in a state of competition. We desire what our neighbor desires. Soon, even the object of desire is forgotten and the competition itself becomes the object of focus. This competition obviously causes a crisis for the community because it threatens to destroy the social order. To resolve this tension, the community finds a scapegoat upon which it can agree to lay the blame for the perceived threat. Once the scapegoat is killed, the tension disappears and the community perceives the victim as manifesting a sacred quality. The victim's death seems to have brought with it renewed life for the community. The victim becomes a part of the mythology of the community that helps to explain the origins of the renewed social order—and is usually represented as a god who dies and is resurrected.[4]

The connection with Christianity is obvious, although Girard notes that the Christian myth does something unique: it recognizes the innocence of the scapegoat (Christ) and refuses to ratify the act of violence against him. Christ is a unique victim because of his teaching and the circumstances around his execution, both of which warn against the dangers of mimetic violence. Jesus is the one human who refrains from violence even in the face of death.[5] Jesus is therefore the most innocent of all victims, which makes the choice of Jesus as scapegoat both inevitable and unjustifiable. The system of sacrifice that has served as the release valve for mimetic competition can no longer hide behind a mythology that justifies its violence. Girard sees the Gospels as providing an account of this unmasking of the sacrificial system.

Unfortunately, Girard says, the original message of the Gospels was soon corrupted and made to function again as a sacrificial text. The book of Hebrews, for instance, leads the way in interpreting Christ's death as a sacrifice to atone for human sin.[6] Christ is compared to a high priest, who offers himself as a sacrifice on behalf of the church: "Therefore he had to become like his brothers and sisters in every respect, so that he might be a merciful and faithful high priest in the service of God, to make a sacrifice of atonement for the sins of the people" (2:17). Sacrifice later became a major category for understanding atonement, especially in Protestant discourse.

These sacrificial interpretations respond to the superficial resemblance between Christ and other scapegoated victims, but miss the most important element, which is that responsibility for that violence is placed on humans, not God.[7] This is why the Gospels have not resulted in a widespread change in human culture, and in fact have been used against their original impulse to found a new culture just as sacrificial as before. The only difference now is that the Gospels, containing the seed of the unmasking of sacrificial systems, have begun to erode the ability of violence to contain itself. This may actually result in a multiplication of violence, at least until there is a widespread realization of its futility.[8]

In Girard's understanding, Christ is no longer a sacrifice and therefore no longer "sacred."[9] He says, "I think that it is necessary to rid ourselves of the sacred, for the sacred plays no part in the death of Jesus."[10] Girard interprets the Christian claim of the divinity of Jesus as referring to a potential that all humans have of relinquishing the cycle of mimetic violence. Jesus is God because he behaves in a uniquely divine manner—he is free from any stain of the founding violence.[11] Girard's theory is therefore both naturalistic and orthodox—Jesus is fully human and fully divine.

Shortcomings in Girard

While Girard's theory accounts for the nonviolent impulses of Christianity, he does so only by ignoring certain elements of Christian self-interpretation. Even if, as Girard claims, "in the first years of Christianity there existed a rigorous (though not yet explicit) intuition of the logic determining the gospel text," early Christians still had a very different picture of Christ than Girard offers. In particular, the idea of Christ as "Lord" poses a problem for Girard because it introduces the idea of sovereignty.

The connection between sovereignty and sacrifice is well developed in Girard's writing. According to Girard, the monarch is simply a reiteration of the sacrificial victim. The community always seeks to reproduce the efficacy of the scapegoat, and the scapegoat is the one who is endowed with the superhuman ability to destroy and create order. As Girard says, "One must look to this prestige as the source for all political and religious sovereignty."[12] Monarchy develops out of sacrifice as the interval between the selection of the scapegoat and his or her death is prolonged. This interval allows the victim to consolidate power and eventually make any actual act of violence against the victim impossible. The king is therefore a sacrificial victim who has indefinitely deferred his execution. "The spirit of kingship is the unanimous reconciliation that occurred spontaneously at the expense of a victim the king is now called upon to replace."[13] Part of the function of sovereignty, therefore, is to demand total loyalty from its subjects to bring about the social order promised by sacrifice.

Girard would probably ask us to interpret the early Christian imputation of sovereignty to Christ in the same way that we would interpret the passion narrative—as parallel to a sacrificial narrative but with key differences.[14] However, in this case there are several difficulties. For instance, the Gospels themselves make use of Christ's sovereignty in a more straightforward way than Christ's sacrifice. Girard could legitimately argue that the sacrificial interpretation was a later corruption of the original Christian message, but the sovereignty of Christ appears to be an essential feature of the Gospels themselves. For instance, the gospel of Matthew is written so as to portray Jesus in the line of Jewish kings. Several of Paul's letters, even those thought to be authentic, contain the formula "Jesus is Lord."[15] The word *Christ* itself (meaning "anointed") points back to the ceremonies for installing the ancient kings of Israel and Judah. The development of the "sacraments" mirrored the *sacramentum*, an oath of allegiance that Roman soldiers made to the emperor and the gods.[16] So the symbol of Christ as sovereign was probably one of the earliest intuitions of the church. And unlike the parallels to sacrifice in the Gospels, there is no hint that the early church wanted to undermine the concept of sovereignty itself. Certainly Christ was supposed to be an alternative to the sovereignty of Caesar, but this in no way reduced the concept of Christ's own sovereignty. The church owed to Christ their total loyalty.

The early Christian idea of sovereignty is a problem not only for Girard, because it would challenge his claim to have found the original meaning of the Gospels, but also in practice, because it undermines the ability of the Christ symbol to motivate a resistance to violence. If Christ is not sacred, as Girard would have it, and therefore not a sovereign, then he is simply an innocent victim, deserving of pity or compassion but not loyalty. The difference in language here signifies a difference in the degree of one's stance against systems of violence, such as the scapegoating mechanism. If one's objection to this system comes only as a response to an example of injustice (i.e., the story of the crucifixion in the Gospels), the compassion one feels may result in resistance up to a point but will not demand a total commitment to its eradication. This is precisely because total commitment is related to the concept of sovereignty: only a sovereign can demand of its citizens loyalty to the point of self-sacrifice.

Kahn's Proposal

A similar problem arises in the work of Paul Kahn, who locates the origins of violence in the sovereign's demand for sacrifice. In his book *Sacred Violence*, Kahn argues that the capacity of American society to permit torture is a result of the strength of the concept of sovereignty. Unlike law, which seeks universal well-being for individuals, sovereignty demands absolute loyalty from its subjects at the expense of those beyond its borders. To defend its own identity, the sovereign demands a sacrifice that transcends the ordinary purview of law. The sovereign may therefore command a subject to kill or be killed on behalf of the political body. In democracies, the monarchical sovereign has been replaced by popular sovereignty, but this does not change the basic relationship between the individual citizen and the state, which can in principle draft its citizens and command them to kill or die on its behalf.[17] In fact, it is only when the sovereign has the ability to demand such a sacrifice, Kahn suggests, that it can truly sustain political identity.[18]

Torture is one particularly interesting example for Kahn because it illustrates the dilemma of the liberal state. On one hand, the state is committed to the universal principles of the law, which clearly prohibit the cruel and unusual types of violence that are usually defined as torture. On the other hand, torture is merely an extension of the logic of the battlefield—we seek to dominate the enemy to prove the power of the sovereign—and therefore we can hardly blame those who participate in torture without also indicting the entire system of warfare upon which political sovereignty is based.[19] We can never quite solve this dilemma; instead we try to hide our use of torture as best we can and scapegoat those most directly involved when these practices come to light.

Although Kahn is pessimistic about escaping from the paradigm of sovereignty, he opposes its parochial violence with that of international law, which attempts to provide for universal well-being apart from any particular national or ethnic identity. There are, for instance, humanitarian projects that do not demand sacrifice from their participants and therefore do not participate in systems of war and torture.

> We may loosely speak of "sacrificing oneself for others" when we mean participation in public interest projects, both here and abroad. Admirable as these projects are, the meaning of sacrifice here has nothing to do with . . . literal self-sacrifice. . . . Indeed, just the opposite, for these are generally projects founded on a cosmopolitan idea of law and a universal conception of material well-being, not the killing and being killed of sacrificial politics.[20]

Kahn holds universal law as an ideal that exists in tension with the realities of political sovereignty. Perhaps, he says, we might one day transcend nationalism in favor of a cosmopolitan identity, but this will only happen when states cease to feel threatened. In a world of terrorism and nuclear weapons, this seems like a distant dream indeed.[21]

Kahn notes that the tension between law and sovereignty can be symbolized by the respective figures of Abraham and Christ. Abraham is the paradigmatic example of the one who sacrifices on behalf of a sovereign in the construction of a particular identity. He leaves home and family at the request of his God and is even willing to literally sacrifice Isaac, his only son, when God commands it. On the other hand, Christ is the example of universal love that transcends particularity and extends goodwill irrespective of borders. As Kahn says, "The Western nation-state exists in a tension between the particularity of Abraham and the universality of Christ."[22] We hold Christ's vision of universal justice and love as our ideal, but we cannot escape our own particularity, our willingness to kill and be killed to defend our sovereignty against other competing claims.

Shortcomings in Kahn

Although Kahn takes a nuanced view of the relationship between the discourses of international law and nationalism, his acceptance of universality as an ideal prevents him from seeing the way that the Western project of universality may also contribute to the violence of particularity. Here Talal Asad's analysis of terrorism is helpful. Asad notes that the definition of "terrorism" versus "combat" depends on a prior, arbitrary distinction between civilized and uncivilized societies. He says that

it is not cruelty that matters in the distinction between terrorists and armies at war, still less the threat that each poses to entire ways of life, but their civilizational status. What is really at stake is not a clash of civilizations . . . but the fight of civilization against the uncivilized.[23]

Asad shows that the norms that are constructed as universal (e.g., human rights, international law, etc.) may actually be used to perpetuate the ability of one group of people to use extreme force against another group. This distinction transcends national boundaries; we consider Western nations to be civilized and therefore improper targets of excessive retaliation or torture. Only those who fail to cooperate with this universal vision, who usually (and conveniently) happen to have skin tones in the brown or black spectrum, are appropriate victims in the "war on terror."

In fact, Kahn's distinction between universal law and particular sovereignty is a false one. The most cosmopolitan vision can end up demanding sacrifice as much as or more than the national sovereign.[24] In fact, by promoting a loyalty to universal principles, one may create a sovereign that extends beyond the traditional borders of a nation. The result is a potential for even broader violence, this time directed against any who refuse to act by the norms of "civilization."

Both Girard and Kahn make use of the symbol of Christ to respond to the existence of sacrificial violence, but both fail in certain respects because of their separation of Christ and sovereignty. Clearly, Girard and Kahn show the desirability of making such a separation, since sovereignty is so closely related to violence, but each of them allows violence to sneak back into their systems. In Girard, the denial of the sacredness of Christ undermines the ability of that symbol to motivate resistance to violence. In Kahn, the universality of Christ masks the potential of that universal to set itself up as a sovereign of sovereigns, ushering in new modes of violence that are even more difficult to resist because they seem more justifiable.

To transcend systems of violence, it is not enough to simply deny the sovereignty that founds political community. By itself, this merely produces either the insipid cosmopolitanism that withdraws, as Kahn notes, in the face of any serious threat,[25] or the militant defense of a universal ethos that only mimics the national sovereign on a broader scale. Instead, it is necessary to turn the concept of sovereignty inside out, so that the sovereign maintains its ability to demand, but represents those excluded from the political community rather than inside it. This requires a radical shift in identity since the sovereign can no longer be grasped as a symbol of a distinct group. In fact, the sovereign now represents the space outside of one's own identity. This is a sovereign who requires loyalty on behalf of enemies, not against them. This is the sovereignty, or rather non/sovereignty, that the Gospels attribute to Christ.

One of the main features of sovereignty is its asymmetry, and Christian sovereignty is no different in this respect. Kahn himself nearly stumbles onto this. He remarks earlier in his book that sovereignty is characterized by the asymmetry of war, as opposed to the symmetry of legal rights: "As a set of legal rules, humanitarian law demands that each side in a conflict recognize the same rights and duties. But combat, as an activity of killing and being killed, moves according to a logic of asymmetry: each side seeks the advantage."[26] Later, he says that Christ also functions asymmetrically, although here he uses this to contrast Christ with the logic of sovereignty.[27] It would be more consistent to realize that Christ represents a form of sovereignty but has reversed the asymmetry; now the nonmember is prioritized over the member of the community.

Political Theology according to Hubmaier

As noted before, the sacraments were originally seen as alternatives to the Roman method of binding a citizen or soldier to the sovereign. Similarly, the role of Christian sacraments in general is to mediate sovereignty to the faith community. In particular, baptism and the Eucharist were the main rituals through which Christians expressed their philosophies of sovereignty, both religious and political. We have seen (in chapter 2) how Reformation leaders fiercely debated the fine points of the Eucharist, and this is because the ritual not only defined issues of ecclesial or social belonging, but also political allegiance. At stake in these debates was the nature of sovereignty and the nature of human relationships to sovereignty. Changes in the Reformation Eucharist foreshadowed major changes in the socio-political structure of Europe.

> The rejection of the priestly role of ritual mediation between parishioner and God was not a rejection of the symbolism of the body of Christ as the community of the Church. Participation in that body, however, was now immediate. Christ was an immediate presence requiring no external ritual but only an inward turning. So it is with popular sovereignty.[28]

The American and French revolutions were applications of the sacramental theology of magisterial Protestantism.

Hubmaier's version of the Eucharist represents a political path not taken. More than the magisterial rituals, Hubmaier's Eucharist maintains the form of non/sovereignty associated with the Christ of the empty tomb, through the idea of the absence of Christ in the elements and reappearance in the marginalized. Hubmaier believed that the referent of the Eucharist—the body of Christ—was the faith community itself, and specifically the ethical relations of the community. In other words, God is mediated to the community only in and through an ethical response to the neighbor.[29] Belonging is inseparable from an action of love for others, even and especially sacrificial love (since sovereignty and sacrifice are intimately connected). For Hubmaier, sovereignty is experienced as that which is vulnerable and therefore in some sense exists outside of the communal identity.[30]

One of the consequences of Hubmaier's sacramental theology is that the Anabaptist definition of sovereignty is inherently unstable. As soon as the sovereign, in the form of the marginal or vulnerable, is successfully mediated to the community, it ceases to represent sovereignty. Therefore, a political community with an external sovereign must have a nomadic identity, at best. It would be an identity that flows against traces of sovereignty rather than ever being able to possess or define it. Perhaps, instead of a path not taken, Anabaptist sacramentology has always haunted Western civilization as well, always at the edges of the magisterial theologies. We might catch a glimpse of this sacramentology in the drift and crisis of modern institutions, both political and ecclesiological.

Christ as sovereign is dissolved into the external. Phenomenologically, this means that the Christian meets his or her sovereign in the neighbor, especially the marginalized neighbor. The distinction between sovereign and enemy collapses as the king is manifested not just as an absence but as immanentized in the other. Christ can, without contradiction, serve as "Lord" and also as outcast, as expressed in the parable of the sheep and the goats in Matthew: "And the king will answer them, 'Truly I tell you, just as you did it to one of the least of these who are members of my family, you did it to me.'"[31] The story loses its power either if the king were not truly sovereign (did not have authority), or if the king were not truly identified with the hungry, the stranger, and the imprisoned.

Using Girard's definition of sacrifice, Christ does indeed represent an end to the sacrificial system. That is, Christ makes impossible the violence against the scapegoat that produces group cohesion. But this is accomplished *through* sovereignty and sacrifice, not by escaping them altogether. Precisely because of the demand for sacrifice (in the sense of ultimate loyalty) that comes from the outside, Christ's non/sovereignty destabilizes identity boundaries and borders, so that sacrificial loyalty works counter to the communal identity instead of maintaining it.

There is a reason that early Christian pacifism emerged out of a church that confessed "Jesus is Lord." The demand of Christ's non/sovereignty is always toward nonviolence, since the loyalty which was once reserved for the state now lies with those who could be potential objects of our violence due to our identification with some community. War becomes a type of treason in the Christian paradigm, even more serious than the usual form of treason because there is by definition no hope of establishing a legitimate government in the place of the current one. The act of establishment is precisely what would make it un-Christian.

The early Christians experienced the absence of Jesus as eliciting and even requiring new communal forms of creativity. But they also experienced Christ as sovereign, that is, as ultimate demand. This collapse of sovereignty into emptiness subverts the very idea of political identity as it has functioned in the West. Christ's sovereignty, as considered in and through the symbol of the empty tomb, cannot be stabilized within a particular authority figure, and therefore cannot be contained within any social boundary. Rather, Christian sovereignty is always displaced beyond social borders and appears to those within the borders as a challenging, foreign presence. Christ as king is Christ as enemy; the one who cannot be incorporated into a community.

SIX

THE REELING EARTH: ECO-THEOLOGY IN THE ABSENCE OF CHRIST

Every creature seems like God and God's anger, even though it be but a
rustling leaf... we do not stand in awe of God's anger but remain unmoved,
and yet we fear and flee from the anger of a frail, withered leaf.
—Martin Luther[1]

We have seen how the empty tomb represents both a space and a demand in regard to human relations. It represents the priority of relations over substance or identity in the structure of self and universe and affects the location of authority or sovereignty within those structures. So far we have mainly considered implications for human selves and communities, but in fact as a metaphysical framework, divine absence might play as much of a role in the natural world, including but not limited to human relations with the rest of nature. A theology informed by the empty tomb is better able to avoid the twin pitfalls of anthropocentrism and romanticism, both of which mask the concrete interdependence of humans and the earth. The empty tomb points us back to a materialist, but not mechanistic, view of the natural world.

The Problem with Values

The problem of anthropocentrism is the easier of the two to identify, although difficult to overcome in practice. Much of our philosophical and religious tradition does indeed assume the priority or uniqueness of human beings over against the rest of nature. We have assumed that the natural world is created for our use, that humans are ultimately more permanent or real than nature, and that religion is really about our internal state rather than our relationship with an external environment. It can be tempting then to try to reject critical theory completely and instead focus on a new set of ecological values.

Certainly, our values shape the way we think about ourselves, treat others, use resources. It is natural to think that our ecological crisis is a crisis of values, that the ecological crisis can be addressed through new theological metaphors and arguments. Back in the 1980s, the pioneering eco-theologian, Sallie McFague, gave us three new models for "an ecological, nuclear age": God as mother, God as lover, and God as friend.[2] Each of these images was meant to counter the monarchical or patriarchal image of God that had long served as the model and justification for human domination of nature. Countless other theological projects outline the biblical basis for ecological ethics, often rooted in the creation story of Genesis or, less often, the psalms that describe reverence for God and nature or the incarnation of God as a flesh-and-blood Jesus.

The values-based approach, however, feeds into the second major problem of ecological theology: romanticization. While anthropocentrism devalues the non-human world, romanticization prevents us from getting an accurate picture of the complexities of our physical environment. An overly romantic eco-theology ends up assigning some kind of teleology to nature, perhaps a divine purpose or organization that we should consider sacred. We talk about balance or sustainability as if it were an unchanging feature of the natural world, and that the primary task is to recommit ourselves to such a divine order.

However, even a superficial look at the disciplines of natural science shows that the teleological view is misleading. Nature, just as much as human society, is in the grip of contingent historical circumstances. Organisms have long-term, permanent effects on their environment, and vice versa, and there is no consistent equilibrium that God has ordained for the world. We are in the middle of a long process of dynamic coevolution, and we cannot understand nature without analyzing its physical history, just as human society is incomprehensible without some understanding of its historical development.

The romanticization of nature is not just a problem for Christians or theologians but for the discipline of environmental science in general. John Bellamy Foster complains that we spend much energy debating environmental issues but have made little progress. He puts most of the blame on Green theory and deep ecology, which reject the Western scientific and philosophical tradition as anthropocentric. But by creating a romantic, vitalist portrait of nature, we have cut ourselves off from exploring the historical trajectory that brought us to our current crisis. Foster says,

> The ecological question is reduced first and foremost to one of *values*, while the much more difficult issue of understanding the *evolving material interrelations* . . . between human beings and nature is thereby missed altogether. . . . Approaches that focus simply on ecological *values*, like philosophical idealism and spiritualism more generally, are of little help in understanding these complex relations."[3]

The New Materialism

Instead, many recent theologians have advocated a "new materialism," which means paying attention to the relationship of humans to their physical surroundings and the history of that relationship over time. Yes, values are important, but values are always embedded in a material context and emerge out of a specific interplay of material causes. It's important to note that philosophical materialism is not the same as being "materialistic" in the usual sense. In fact, Joerg Rieger points out that those who we think of as "materialistic" are often driven by abstract concerns, like social belonging, prestige, love, or comfort. Advertisers are usually focused on selling an idea more than a physical product; a Coke means belonging to a happy, laughing family; a BMW means enjoying the nightlife with your glamorous romantic interest. In the philosophical sense, then, what we usually call materialism is actually a form of idealism, where the idea or value takes precedence over the object.[4]

Materialism also does not necessarily imply determinism. Just because our values arise in a physical and historical context does not mean that we play no active role in shaping our choices and our future. We are limited and shaped by our context, but we also in turn shape our surroundings in material ways. True materialism, as Henri Lefebvre defines it,

> determines the practical relations inherent in every organised human existence and studies them inasmuch as they are concrete conditions of existence for cultures or ways of life. The simple relations, moments and categories are involved, historically and methodologically, in the richer and more complex determinations, but they do not exhaust them. The given content is always a concrete totality. This complex content of life and consciousness is the true reality which we must attain and elucidate."[5]

In theological discussions, we tend to exaggerate the influence that our religious values have on the way we live and to miss the influence our material context has on our religious values. Rieger says,

> The benefit of dialectical materialisms is that they remind us that religious experience is not only complex and shaped by various ideal and material influences; it is also shaped by particular interests and powers whose effectiveness increases the more they operate underground and out of sight.[6]

The point is not that we should abandon discourse about values in general, nor that abstract philosophical or theological thinking is necessarily anti-ecological. Materialism itself is, after all, a philosophy, and one that has deep roots in the Christian tradition. Rather, we need to ask *which kind* of theology encourages the kind of concrete analysis of material relations that actually helps us understand and respond constructively to ecological problems. Here we need to turn back again to the idea of the sacrament as the basic religious category that expresses the location of sacredness in the material world. Specifically, we can trace the development of Marx's philosophy, the most influential modern variety of materialism, back through Hegel to Luther and the sacramental debates of the sixteenth century.

Luther and Hegel

Remember that, particularly in the Reformation, sacraments functioned as social expressions of basic philosophical and theological commitments, which made them the locus of fierce disagreements. Sacraments were not just formal rituals; they were propositions about how the sacred relates to the world, how it is embodied in the world, and who controls this process. Luther's sacramentology—a combination of objective elements and human subjectivity—affects the way he thinks about the non-human world. It is in his sacramental theology that Luther affirms nature most strongly as a revelation of God: "[God] must be present in every single creature in its innermost and outermost being, on all sides, through and through, below and above, before and behind, so that nothing can be more truly present and within all creatures than God himself with his power."[7] He sees in a mouse, for instance, evidence of the intricacies of creation and a divine plan.[8] At times, his sympathy for other animals leads him to practical advocacy; he once tried to save a baby rabbit during a hunt (sadly, his effort was thwarted by the overeager hunting dogs).[9]

At the same time, Luther is careful to maintain an unbridgeable distance between creation and God, and between humans and other animals. Luther clearly has an anthropocentric view of creation: the natural world is created for humans, and humans remain dominant over the rest of nature. Thorns, thistles, and flies exist to punish human sin.[10] While he recognizes the continuity between humans and other animals, Luther believes that human animality exists to humble us; when we compare ourselves with cows or donkeys, it produces such anxiety in us that we are driven to the Genesis story to find proof of our superiority.[11] On the whole, Luther's ecological thought might include empathy with other creatures, but it fails in both respects noted above: it is anthropocentric *and* romanticizes nature.[12]

Luther's sacramental theology left a deep mark on Western philosophy. Hegel, for instance, identified as a Lutheran and considered Luther's theology to be a major influence. Just as Luther experienced the objective Eucharist to be an obstacle to the human experience of the sacred and so developed a theology to internalize the Eucharist, Hegel developed a philosophy in which the sacred is developed in history through the reconciliation of the external and the internal. Hegel himself clearly recognized his debt to Luther and was explicit about the connections between Luther's sacramental theology and his own dialectical philosophy:

> Each [individual] has to accomplish the work of reconciliation in his own Soul—Subjective Spirit has to receive the Spirit of Truth

into itself, and give it a dwelling place there. . . . Subjectivity therefore made the objective purport of Christianity, i.e., the doctrine of the Church, its own. In the Lutheran Church the subjective feeling and the conviction of the individual is regarded as equally necessary with the objective side of Truth."[13]

Essentially, Hegel took the structure of the Lutheran Eucharist and applied it to philosophical metaphysics. For Luther, the external substance of the elements is subjectified by the Christian and reconciled with their own identity. For Hegel, the entire world is in the process of being subsumed in a larger process of reconciliation, which he calls absolute Spirit. A problem arises when this process is blocked, when an objective thing is set up and worshiped as sacred in itself. Hegel used the medieval Catholic sacrament as an analogy here: "The most prominent feature in this sacrament [the illegitimate sacrament] is, that the process by which Deity is manifested, is conditioned by the limitations of particularity—that the Host, this *Thing*, is set up to be adored as God."[14] When the sacred is objectified and remains external, then the subject is alienated from the sacred. The priests control the Eucharist and can provide it or deny it to participants at will.

Like Luther, Hegel's philosophy leads him to a qualified appreciation of the material, non-human world. On the one hand, nature, considered as an objective reality separate from human consciousness, is a necessary part of the movement toward absolute Spirit. The evolution of human thought inevitably leads to the realization that, from a larger vantage point, we are inseparable from nature. On the other hand, the role of nature in Hegel's system is to serve the movement of consciousness, which is most fully realized in human beings. Nature has no history or development of its own[15] but is subordinate to the development of Spirit, manifested most fully in human civilization and crowned by the emergence of art, religion, and especially philosophy. Like Luther, then, nature has an essential role to play, but ultimately only within a framework of human development.

Marx's Sacramentology

One of the main critics of Hegel's system, of course, was Karl Marx. Marx picked up on the topic of alienation, but he applied it to an economic rather than ideological framework. Marx recognizes the same patterns appearing in economic relations that appeared in medieval religion; in fact, he insists that one can only understand capitalism by analogy to religion.

> A commodity appears at first sight an extremely obvious, trivial thing. But its analysis brings out that it is a very strange thing, abounding in metaphysical subtleties and theological niceties. . . . In order, therefore, to find an analogy we must take flight into the misty realm of religion. There the products of the human brain appear as autonomous figures endowed with a life of their own, which enter into relations both with each other and with the human race. . . . I call this the fetishism which attaches itself to the products of labor as soon as they are produced as commodities, and is therefore inseparable from the production of commodities.[16]

As Andrew Cole says, the commodity is the modern version of the Eucharist, both of which, in Marx's opinion, embody and justify uneven social relations.[17]

The difference between Hegel and Marx is that Hegel believes the alienation between the subject and its external environment can be overcome by sacramental identification of the two. The Lutheran mass is effective, according to Hegel, because of the union of my subjective faith and the objective reality of the Eucharist. Hegel calls this "feeling"—it's the "something more" that makes differences disappear between a person and an external thing.[18] But for Marx, "feeling" is just as much a part of the problem, just as much a form of "fetishism" as the reified sacrament that Hegel denounced.[19] When social relations are embodied in commodities, the real relations among humans and between humans and nature are disguised. Marx believes that we must uncover social relations first to understand our reality.

With respect to ecology, the most interesting implication of Marx's "sacramentology" is that nature is allowed to take on a life of its own, not merely in service to human ends, and also not as a vehicle for romanticized values. While Marx certainly focuses on human economic relationships, he considers the relations between humans and the natural world to be part of the same materialist plane. Marx is therefore able to consider that the natural world has an objective material history of its own, which affects and is affected by human actions. Therefore, Marx believed that natural science, like social science, would have to begin with an empirical analysis of material relations and that the negative impact of human behavior on the natural world could be analyzed and changed.

The solution to the alienation of human beings from nature, Marx insisted, was to be discovered only in the realm of practice, in human history. The self-alienation of human beings both from human species-being and from nature, which constituted so much of human history, also found its necessary resolution, in that same human history, through the struggle to transcend this human self-alienation.[20]

In summary, the disagreement between Hegel and Marx might be seen as a repetition of the sixteenth-century debates about the Eucharist and Marx's version of dialectical materialism as a secularized sacramental theology. And each way of expressing the relationship between the sacred and the world affects the development of ecological ethics.

Anabaptist Eco-Theology

If Hegel represents the Lutheran idea of the sacrament, an Anabaptist eco-theology might play the same theological role as Marx. Hubmaier, like the other reformers, was reacting against the Catholic idea of the Eucharist as an objective presentation of the sacred. But he was also reacting against the Lutheran and the Zwinglian Eucharist: the Lutheran idea being that Christ was physically present in the Eucharist although its efficacy depended on the subjective faith of the participant. Ulrich Zwingli, the Swiss reformer who influenced many early Anabaptists, thought of the Eucharist as a memorial of a past event. Christ is not present in the bread and wine but becomes symbolically present in the congregation as they remember Christ's sacrifice.

As noted in chapter 2, Hubmaier agreed with Zwingli in many respects, but rather than thinking of the Eucharist as mediating a symbolic change in the psychology of the participants, he believed that the Eucharist mediates an external, ontological change. In other words, the sacred is manifested in the world only through a concrete ethical response to the Eucharist. Christ is made present in the material relations between the Christian and the world.

In practice, Anabaptist theology did not develop into a critical ecological ethics. We might perhaps excuse the sixteenth-century Anabaptists on the grounds that the idea of humans having a significant effect
on the entire natural order would be anachronistic to the time period.
But even when compared to their contemporaries, Anabaptists limited
their sacramental theology more strictly to humans and the human
community. Though Anabaptists had successfully migrated the sacred
to the community of believers, they were not successful in imagining
how the sacred might be expressed in non-human relations. Instead, the
dualism of church and society was usually extended to a dualism between spiritual and material reality.[21] Heather Bean writes, "Anabaptist
theology has been impeded by this understanding of the created world
as the realm of Satan separate from God and believers, by anthropocentrism, and by the absence of a clear doctrine of creation."[22]

So the problem of Anabaptist neglect of ecology is not merely one
of historical milieu but has to do with the way that Anabaptist theology
was developed and applied. Karl Koop rightly recognizes,

> If we were to take the time to contemplate the longer view, the
> "Long Reformation" of Anabaptism, we would most certainly
> see a continuation of this tradition, less attentive to the natural
> and material world, and more deeply invested in anthropological
> and ecclesiological concerns.[23]

However, we should not conclude that the basic impulse behind
Anabaptist sacramental theology, the impulse to locate the sacred in
communal relations, is anti-ecological. The solution is not to somehow
reverse the Reformation to retrieve the earlier medieval idea of objective
divine presence in the natural world. That would perhaps address the
problem of anthropocentrism, but it would exacerbate the problem of
romanticization, arguably the more tempting pitfall for ecologically
minded people today.[24] Rather, the problem is one of incomplete mi-
gration of the sacred in the Radical Reformation. The fundamental absence of Christ in the Eucharist must be extended to a fundamental,
metaphysical absence at the heart of creation, one that elicits and points
our attention back to the relations between all creatures.

In the same way that Hegel extended Luther's sacramental theology
to a broader philosophy about the world, Anabaptists today might draw
on theological resources like Hubmaier to articulate how the sacred and

the environment are related in the Anabaptist worldview. And in the same way that Marx "turned Hegel on his head" by changing the focus from ideology to economic relations, we should recognize Hubmaier's theology as turning Luther's sacrament on its head by changing the focus from individual subjectivity to objective, material relations. Consider Marx's description of the difference between himself and Hegel:

> In direct contrast to German philosophy, which descends from heaven to earth, here we ascend from earth to heaven. That is to say, we do not set out from what men say, imagine, conceive, nor from men as narrated, thought of, imagined, conceived, to arrive at men in the flesh. We set out from real, active men, and on the basis of their real life process we demonstrate the development of the ideological reflexes and echoes of this life process. . . . Ideology has no history, no development; but men, developing their material production and their material intercourse, alter, along with this, their real existence, their thinking, and the products of their thinking. Life is not determined by consciousness, but consciousness by life.[25]

Similarly, Hubmaier and other Anabaptists point toward an empirical faith that grows out of the material relations of the community to the environment. We do not look for the sacred in the abstract and then try to apply it to nature. Rather, we should try to uncover our actual relationships to our environment and, through that analysis and our ethical response, discover sacredness. There is no ultimate reality behind nature that we could point to apart from the concrete web of relationships where we find ourselves. Our ecological relations, no less than human relations, emerge within and are motivated by an absence of the divine.

Bioregionalism as Materialist Eco-Theology

A materialist eco-theology has much in common with the existing movement of bioregionalism. Bioregionalism portrays human communities as a part of their natural context and points us toward an understanding of our environment in its concrete form rather than in the abstract. Ched Myers, for instance, claims that Mennonite theology needs to take into account the actual watershed where the church community lives, the local animal and plant species, the energy used to heat and light the building, the economic ties that define the church's relationship to its city. "Only a grounded incarnational faith can battle the placeless theological docetism of modernity with its abstract rationalism and idealist ethics."[26] Yet the image of the incarnation can be problematic unless it is preceded by an image of the tomb; there is a subtle but important difference between identifying God with "nature," and identifying God as the space within which creaturely relationships (natural and human) emerge. One sees even in bioregionalism the temptation to see "nature" in overly romantic terms, perhaps by assuming that the non-human natural order provides an automatic blueprint for human ethics.

At its best, though, bioregionalism is not simply about reconnecting to an ideal landscape, romanticized as a source of value independent from or immune to human impact. Rather, bioregionalism includes learning and responding to the history of one's place, which is always a confluence of natural history and socio-political history. As Myers says, "Central to a watershed ethos should be a commitment to restorative justice for all those displaced in the past and marginalized in the present. The land itself is an historic subject whose story must be learned."[27] If the land is developing its own history, producing, destroying, and replacing networks of relations, then the natural order is just as contingent as the human order and requires just as nuanced an interpretation as social and political structures.

Thus the non-human world also presents us with a Levinasian "face" in that it is constituted by unique, asymmetrical, and transcendent relations. Under an Anabaptist understanding of sacraments, our environment becomes a vehicle for the sacred insofar as power shapes the relations of all forms of life—in other words, not because God is automatically present in nature but because the dynamic of divine absence and presence functions just as much there as in human relations. As Martin Luther unwittingly suggested, in the Anthropocene era, we might encounter the transcendence of God in starving polar bears, bleached coral, and withered leaves.

SEVEN

THE CLEANNESS OF MY HANDS: TOPOGRAPHICAL PACIFISM

If I had known what blankness would ultimately surround me when I began the task, perhaps I would have chosen to remain behind these walls of secure meditation and not address myself to the discovery of the world. . . . My map absorbs me with what it does not reveal. Each time I gaze upon it I am captivated by what so far has not been included within its margins. . . . Grant me strength, O Lord, to venture forth into a region that as yet has not been revealed.
—Fra Mauro, in James Cowan's *The Mapmaker's Dream*[1]

The absent Christ is not available as a dogmatic foundation for Christian pacifism, though hopefully it is already apparent that divine absence might ground a commitment to nonviolence, both politically and ecologically. This final chapter begins to describe a pacifist aesthetics within our relational metaphysics, in which objects are constituted by a landscape of relations.

The ethical task is then something more like mapmaking, tracing the contours of power that define oneself and one's place in the world. But mapmaking is an art, a product of social judgments. The best maps are not only geographically accurate; in some cases they may even be less geographically accurate than other versions, but they reveal some pattern in the world that was not apparent before. So pacifism is less about a specific set of behaviors and more about discovering and expressing new patterns within our material relations. Pacifism means cultivating an inexhaustibly creative stance toward one's social and environmental context.

We begin with a reflection on one of the most famous maps ever drawn: John Snow's map of the London cholera epidemic of 1854. The effectiveness of a map like Snow's is based on the same characteristics that make any abstraction effective: selective presentation of facts, attention to outliers, and interpretation within a social context. In the same way, the social construction of the network of relations that constitute the self is necessarily an abstraction from a totality that can never be fully captured. It therefore cannot avoid gaps that are potentially violent—but it also offers infinite opportunities for reconstituting relations in less violent ways.

John Snow's Cholera Map

In 1854, there was a cholera epidemic in London, "the most terrible . . . which ever occurred in this kingdom."[2] In what has now become cartographical legend, the English physician John Snow used a map to represent the causal connection between cholera deaths and the contaminated water pump handle on Broad Street, definitively proving that cholera is transmitted through water instead of air.

Before the epidemic, Snow had hypothesized that cholera was water-borne, but he was having trouble convincing his colleagues, some of whom believed that cholera rose up from graves of previous plague victims and lingered in the air.[3] When cholera broke out around Broad Street, Snow received a list of eighty-three (out of about 500) deaths from the General Register Office. With this data, he walked the neighborhood interviewing family members of the deceased. Rather than simply graphing a time series of deaths, he plotted each one on a street map of the neighborhood, one dot per death, along with the location of thirteen water pumps.

Snow found that nearly all of the deaths took place within a short distance of one particular water pump, and his interviews confirmed that nearly all the victims had recently collected water from this same pump. There were a few deaths reported from a greater distance away, but several of these people turned out to have also visited the Broad Street pump for one reason or another. On the other hand, Snow noticed a workhouse and a brewery in Broad Street that seemed to have been spared, a fact that worked against his theory. On visiting these places, however, Snow discovered that both had their own well on the premises, and their inmates or employees did not use the public pump.

Snow brought his map to the officials responsible for the water pump, the Board of Guardians, who promptly ordered the handle to be removed so that the pump could not be used. The epidemic of 1854 soon came to an end (though to be fair, it is possible that the disease had also simply run its course). More importantly, the discovery of the cause of cholera—contamination of the water supply by sewage—resulted in widespread reforms to the sanitation system in England and a sharp decline in cholera outbreaks from then on. Cholera epidemics are now virtually unknown in developed countries.

Edward Tufte, pioneer of the field of data visualization, identifies several reasons why Snow's map was so effective. First, Snow succeeded in contextualizing the data so that it was related to a hypothesis of cause and effect. It was crucial to show the connection between the physical location of the cholera deaths and the location of the local water pumps, a fact that could easily be obscured by looking only at the number of deaths in the region, or even a less detailed map that did not include water sources, street names, and local businesses. Even with the same information, a different map might have led an observer to miss the appropriate conclusion and therefore would not have led to successful intervention.

Also, Snow's analysis was greatly strengthened by his inclusion of anomalies in his data and the explanation or resolution of these anomalies. It would be tempting for Snow to simply dismiss the data that did not fit his theory—the cases of cholera outside of the Broad Street neighborhood and the relative health of the workhouse and brewery populations. Instead, after some careful detective work, these cases ended up providing the strongest evidence for his theory and helped convince public officials to act on Snow's data. "The point is to get it right," reflects Tufte, "not to win the case, not to sweep under the rug all the assorted puzzles and inconsistencies that frequently occur in collections of data."[4]

A map, such as Snow's cholera plot, is a particular configuration of information. It is not merely neutral or objective but suggests a framework for interpreting reality. There are an infinite number of ways to draw a map, even maps of exactly the same territory. One could have highlighted, for example, the location of all cemeteries in the Broad Street neighborhood instead of water pumps, which would have suggested a very different conclusion to the Board of Guardians: in the best case, merely an absence of correlation between the two, or in the worst case a spurious correlation that would have meant wasted time and effort. Maps can take an infinite number of shapes, none of which can be said to be inherently "correct," and yet, in relation to a particular question or situation, there are superior and inferior maps. In the context of the cholera epidemic, Snow's map proved to be effective because it revealed something new about the material conditions of life in Broad Street and suggested a new set of actions and interventions in response to that reality.

Snow's map was drawn to make a specific point, to confirm a theory or bias. This is true of all maps, even the most scientific or seemingly objective.

> Map-making *is* manipulation, a process dependent on authorial background, intent, and perspective. Intention determines which elements of what data set will be included in a map and how the data are symbolized for editorial emphasis. None of these maps are value-free representations of reality, pieces of 'neutral science.' All are self-conscious manipulations of a rich ecology.[5]

Maps are products of social judgments—judgments about what is worth depicting, what categories should be used to divide geographical space, and what methods of mapping are most authoritative.

Cartographic Silences

As social judgments, maps are important not only for what they show, but for what they leave out. A good map is a selective map; it shows information that is relevant to its purpose and omits a huge amount of information not deemed relevant. For instance, when the London subway system was being developed in the late nineteenth century, mapmakers tried to draw subway maps with as much spatial accuracy as possible. They preserved a strict scale so that the subway map could be overlaid on top of a street map. Of course, this meant that in middle of London, the map was dense with stations but very empty toward the edges. In fact, the map was only readable if it zoomed in on London and omitted some of the stations furthest away from the downtown.

In 1933, Harry Beck submitted a proposal for a new subway map, in which all routes were simplified and stylized as vertical or horizontal lines with sharp corners. Consecutive stations were more or less the same distance apart from each other on the map, no matter what the real geographical distance.

Beck's map became the visual standard for modern subway maps, the kind that we are now used to reading without a second thought.[6] Although less "accurate" than previous maps, Beck's map was more useful because it gave readers only the information most relevant for them, i.e., the position of subway stations relative to other stations.

However, "silences" within maps are not always intentional nor benign. In his critical history of cartography, J. B. Harley notes that seventeenth-century mapmakers developed an unconscious set of standards by which maps became both more tidy and more abstract.

> [I]n many of the topographical atlases of early modern Europe . . . much of the character and individuality of local places is absent from the map. Behind the façade of a few standard signs on these atlases, the outline of one town looks much the same as that of the next; the villages are more nearly identical and are arranged in a neat taxonomic hierarchy; woodland is aggregated into a few types; even rivers and streams become reduced into a mere token of reality; objects outside the surveyor's classification of "reality" are excluded.[7]

There is a reason, Harley hypothesizes, that maps became more abstract at precisely the time when the modern state was emerging. The "silence of the unique" helped the control of centralized power over a large area. They serve to "dehumanize" the landscape, to "legitimize and neutralize arbitrary actions in the consciousness of their originators."[8] Later, the same tendency to stereotype landscape on maps served to help the colonization of North America, depicting the landscape as "already tamed," ready and awaiting settlement.[9] We inherit these same assumptions of standardization—we are trained to recognize a blue squiggly line as a river, a black dot as a town, green shading for a forest—but what does it do to our consciousness to think of the physical world in terms of a mere handful of simple shapes and shades?

One might also consider how maps have changed even in recent decades with the rapid dominance of GPS and personal navigation software. To get from point A to point B, we no longer pull out a road map to trace the entire journey in the context of a larger landscape. Rather, we experience reality as radically individualized. Even more than previous types of maps, we are now shown only what is immediately relevant for our personal objectives, and we experience geographical space as even more stylized and abstracted. The extreme selectivity that Google provides is what makes these new maps so useful, but it has the side effect of making people less aware of how physical spaces are related to each other, less able to form a mental map of their own surroundings, and less curious about places that fall outside of their individual routes. We might say that the new standardization of maps is characterized by a "silence of the social," in which geographical context is stripped away in favor of individualistic immediacy.

Finally, there are cartographic silences that suppress minority or "other" populations. One example is the tendency of place-names to reflect the dominant group, particularly in the wake of conquest or revolution. Naming places is a way to demonstrate and maintain power over those who live there. Maps can also emphasize and legitimize class differences. In early modern cartography, towns were given more or less prominence based on the social status of their inhabitants. "The largest . . . pictorial signs on the map turn out to be those associated with feudal, military, legal, or ecclesiastical status."[10]

Class plays a similar determining role in contemporary maps, perhaps even more so now when maps can be generated by algorithms based on social media and purchasing habits. In its most extreme form, the "silence of the other" obliterates entire societies and cultures. Colonial maps show empty land rather than indigenous settlements and borders. European maps of the Americas offered "a promise of free and apparently virgin land," but also "a landscape in which the Indian is silent or is relegated, by means of the maps marginal decoration, to the status of a naked cannibal."[11] One might object that the "silence of the other" is merely an indication of lack of information, but this lack of information is precisely the result of a power gradient between the mapmaker, who is in a position to depict reality with or without familiarity with the subject, and the marginal or subaltern, who can *be* depicted without their own agency. Thus, in what they select and omit, maps maintain and shape power relations.

The Self as a Map

The theological absence that we have traced from the early Christian imagination, the Anabaptist sacrament, and Whiteheadian metaphysics implies a self constituted by a network of relations—a topographical self, a map rather than a singular entity. In the Gospels, the original experience of sacredness comes in the form of the empty tomb, a dynamic spaciousness that sparks the formation of faith communities shaped by relational authority. For the Anabaptists, this same relational demand, in the form of an "empty" sacrament, shapes the identity of its participants. And for Whitehead, reality itself is not a collection of substances, but a network of relations that criss-cross a divine space. In this theological framework, an identity is not something that we possess and carry with us as we travel through space and time. Rather, an identity is something that is produced by our relations and is constantly changing as these relations shift. To inhabit an ego is to survey a map of one's relations, both physical and social.

As a map, a self is not an objective experience of reality but a construction that depends on individual idiosyncrasies and social assumptions. Though we all theoretically begin with the same universe of information, our perceptions of reality become useful only insofar as they are selective and interpreted. We automatically and unconsciously highlight certain facets of our experience and ignore others. Our selves are related to our reality as a map is related to physical geography: we reveal something about the world only by abstracting from a larger reality, unrepresentable in its entirety.[12] Every map is, in the end, a derivative of ultimate blankness.

One can draw an infinite number of maps based on the same landscape, just as one can take an infinite number of perspectives on the same set of experiences. But this does not mean that all interpretations are equally valid or useful. Snow's cholera map was superior in his context because it demonstrated a specific causal relationship and allowed for a practical response. Beck's subway map is superior to previous subway maps because it highlights the order and relative location of stations without getting lost in irrelevant detail. And, although all maps distort reality in some way, some do so unnecessarily or unethically, encouraging inappropriate or even violent responses.

At the same time, it is not possible to fit all maps into the same continuum of quality. One cannot say once and for all that Beck's map is superior or inferior to Snow's map, since they are constructed for different purposes. It is tempting to think of cartography as an attempt to asymptotically approach reality, but this is too one-dimensional. Maps can be critiqued based on the specific contexts in which they are used—which information is relevant, which problems need to be solved, which actions can be produced—but these critiques can come simultaneously from multiple directions.

In Christian theology, then, the same type of evaluation—relative, but not viciously so—applies to the perceptions of the self and community. One has to constantly critique and redraw the maps that precipitate out of the primal, divine absence. One might say that a commitment to Christian life is, most basically, a commitment to cartographical creativity—to be attuned to the absence that haunts our maps and to complexify or simplify them so as to reveal something previously hidden. We cannot avoid abstraction, but we can move between different layers, levels and styles of abstraction.

Mapmaking as Nonviolent Conflict Resolution

Moreover, this drive toward relational creativity has a particular character, though not a particular content. Since maps reflect power relations and tend to show or hide information in violent ways, the urge to uncover hidden relations is an urge toward nonviolence. Christian pacifism, then, is the act of investigating the absences around the contours of our consciousness. What anomalies do not fit our interpretive frameworks? What can we not see because of our positions of power?

Since violence is a means of addressing conflict while remaining within the existing "map" of a conflict, nonviolence is phenomenologically felt as a journey through layers of maps. For example, John Roth, a Mennonite history professor, tells the story of an encounter on a train in which a group of teenagers begin harassing and then physically attacking an elderly, mentally disabled man. Roth's first impulse was outrage and an urge to intervene, violently if need be. But Roth had no experience with physical fighting, was not carrying a gun, and was outnumbered four to one. So, instead, he walked up to the scene, called out a friendly greeting to the old man, slipped in between the attackers and led the man back to his seat.[13]

At the outset, this scenario would strike most people as having no obvious nonviolent solution. Even for Roth, who teaches Anabaptist history and was raised as a pacifist, the first responses that came to his mind were those of violent intervention and the possible necessity of self-defense. As he says, it was a combination of his lack of capacity for violence and an amount of luck that allowed him to respond successfully in the way he did. If he had been carrying a firearm, for instance, or if he had been a karate expert, or if he had not considered nonviolence to be a deep part of his faith, it is likely that a violent response would have appeared necessary to him. Instead, Roth was forced to move beyond the parameters of the conflict as it appeared to him, and this happened largely in an immediate, unconscious way. Roth's actions were the result of a new mapping of the conflict, in which an injustice could be addressed productively.

There is no guarantee that we will find immediate, creative solutions like this in such high-stakes situations. But we can make this more likely by cultivating practices of recognizing and transcending frameworks that underlie conflict. For example, John Winslade and Gerald Monk use "narrative mediation" to work through conflict constructively. Essentially, they ask participants to identify the narratives that have produced and sustained a conflict and then attempt to reframe the conflict in ways that allows productive movement. Part of this process involves a "mapping" of the relative influences of the context upon the participants (How has this conflict affected your personal, work or social life? What has this argument cost you?) and the influence of the participants upon their context (What actions have you taken to diminish the conflict?). "The aim of the exploration at this point is to map the territory in sufficient detail so that small holes in the sway of the conflict can start to be explored."[14] The holes in the conflict map, also called "unstoried experience" or "unique outcomes," can then be used as the basis for a new mapping of the participants' identities and relations.[15]

Mapmaking as Dynamic Pacifism

On the socio-political level, our very conception of violence relies on a particular social map. In the West, our collective map defines two distinct spaces—a secular, public zone and a religious, private zone. The idea of the secular/religious divide is not an objective feature of human society, but emerges out of the self-interpretation of seventeenth-century Europeans. William Cavanaugh explains that the idea of secularity emerges from a desire to overcome the violence of the "Wars of Religion" in the 1600s, which were actually as much about the birth of modern political states as they were about religious identity. However, the emergence of the liberal state was portrayed in the Western self-conception as a triumph over religious, irrational, sectarian violence. The separation of church and state, the story goes, allows for a rational civilization characterized by peace and tolerance. That narrative has had a major influence on international politics, particularly in the relationship between Western nations and the predominantly Islamic Middle East. It becomes very easy for the United States to downplay its own violence as a justified response to uncivilized terrorism, which is a result of the backward religious extremism of Islamic states.[16]

Given the social map that we inherit in the West, then, a thoroughgoing pacifism cannot simply mean avoiding participation in military violence. Though conscientious objection can be a valid way to resist social violence, by itself it does not necessarily change the basic paradigm that produces and justifies state violence. In fact, it may coexist very well with the narrative of the neoliberal state, if one thinks of conscientious objection merely as a religious quirk that the state deigns to tolerate. A film like Mel Gibson's *Hacksaw Ridge*, for example, can easily accommodate the story of a conscientious objector within the glorification of warfare in general. In the film, Desmond Doss, a young Seventh Day Adventist and pacifist, enlists in the army as a combat medic out of patriotic duty but refuses to carry a weapon. During the Battle of Okinawa, he heroically returns again and again to the battlefield to bring back wounded soldiers, and his heroism inspires the other soldiers to press on and eventually win the battle. In this case, pacifism is completely compatible with a nationalist and militaristic narrative that undergirds international warfare. At a deeper level, then, nonviolence requires exposing the myths that make state violence possible in the first place.

Christian pacifists, especially of the Anabaptist variety, have often accepted the prevalent social topography, as long as a small territory can be carved out for themselves. It is not an accident that Anabaptists have been some of the most consistent proponents of pacifism over the past five hundred years—their ecclesiological and sacramental structures allowed them to highlight the nonviolent themes in the New Testament and to translate this emphasis into practice. Unfortunately, however, Anabaptist pacifism emerged in a context of biblical literalism, in which pacifism appeared to certain Anabaptist groups as a self-evident scriptural principle. Instead of linking pacifism to the absence within the sacrament, and the relational identity which it fostered, they saw pacifism as something static that could be attained and grasped. The Anabaptists ended up with a dualistic conceptual map that opposed the pure Christian community to the sinful and fallen world.

The nonviolence that Christ represents is not only manifested in a deconstruction of all forms of violence but also the deconstruction of all specific forms of nonviolence. Mennonite conscientious objection, for example, has made a great contribution to social movements against war and state violence but also has tended to obscure the violence internal to Mennonite communities—sexual abuse and gender hierarchies, complicity in colonization and racism, and blindness to economic privilege. James Reimer is correct that Mennonites have tended to downplay the transcendence of Christ—it is true that Christ cannot be captured in a particular form of nonviolence.[17] But that does not necessarily mean that Christ is beyond or above conceptions of violence and nonviolence, only that Christ represents a deeper form of nonviolence, one that always "insists"[18] as an absence troubling the edges of our ethical frameworks.

As Peter Blum says, this may mean that pacifism is impossible in the sense that it can never be finally achieved. And yet, he suggests the possibility of a "no to violence,"[19] which is a stance rather than a guarantee of success. There is always a certain arbitrariness to the way that we draw a map, but this does not keep us from making improvements, paying attention to silences, adding greater specificity, drawing out deeper connections, promoting new practices.

The task of the church, then, is not necessarily to strive for perfection. In fact, it is better to say that the church must be constantly striving for *im*perfection. In other words, the church must cultivate the ability to encourage and adapt to new practices and concepts that reveal its own flaws and limitations. The Anabaptist concept of a two-kingdom theology needs to be replaced with the recognition of a multiplicity of kingdoms, each representing a different possible mapping of reality. In this infinite-kingdom theology, the goal is not to inhabit a particular space, but to embrace the task of redrawing territories, displacing boundaries, and journeying into the blank spaces on the map.

Mapmaking and Beauty

Finally, there is a converse side to the recognition that violence lurks within every conceptual map. That is, every map also contains an element of truth and beauty. Even those maps that do not correspond at all to physical reality, such as the map at the back of a fantasy novel or the abstract maps of Lordy Rodriguez,[20] may communicate something of value to the reader. In the same way, every perceptual framework deserves some basic level of appreciation, even celebration, as an expression of God. This by no means justifies any act of violence. But if the obliviousness to hidden forms of violence can lead even the most well-meaning system into brutality, the obliviousness to value can produce a brutality of its own. It is only too easy, living in times of climate change, racial tension, or economic disparity, to be cynical of everything around us. As in Foucault's description of modernity, the task of pacifist ethics is rather to cultivate an attitude in which "extreme attention to what is real is confronted with the practice of a liberty that simultaneously respects this reality and violates it."[21] The basic impulse is creative engagement rather than disdain.

I visited St. Peter's Basilica in the Vatican some years ago and, like Martin Luther (or Judas, for a less flattering comparison),[22] my first impulse was to be suspicious. Surely the money that it took to create such grandeur could have been better used. I saw in the beauty of the cathedral evidence of extortion and greed, and there is truth to that perspective. No amount of beauty justifies the aggregation of resources at the expense of others. But also, as I continued to gaze up at the intricate ceiling, the huge stained glass windows, and the marble sculptures scattered liberally around the sanctuary, I had to admit that I was glad that something like St. Peter's could exist in the world, and I came away with a renewed sense of awe and appreciation. To be aware of injustice does not necessarily negate the sensitivity to beauty. The two can coexist, and perhaps in the end require each other.

So, whatever map we create to navigate through the darkness, we produce both beauty and violence. With regard to the latter, the divine absence appears as a deconstructive force. It breaks like waves relentlessly on our consciousness. Particularly in situations of immediate and egregious injustice, it calls us to make merciless revisions, find deeper layers of interpretation, draw clearer lines showing our complicity in systems of violence. But within that divine spaciousness there is also an encouragement to create, despite limitations and mistakes, and to say, "It is good." Without that affirmation, Christian pacifism is simply a journey down an infinite abyss, and no matter how much energy one has at the beginning of an infinite journey, it is eventually exhausted. The practice of nonviolence therefore depends also on the virtues of humility, curiosity and receptivity. We should approach this divine absence with the same "fear and great joy"[22] that the women felt upon discovering the empty tomb, and then proceed to Galilee.

CONCLUSION

The empty tomb is a powerful symbol in Christian theology which expresses a very specific relationship between divine authority and the world. Christ, God's representative and mediator, is not physically present to the world, but precisely because of that absence can be universally claimed in opposition to all other varieties of authority. The empty tomb is a historical, material setting, but its reference is not itself physical.

In the same way, God is defined by and through the material world but is not identical to or contained by the material world. God is neither supernatural (above or apart from nature) nor natural (one part of the world among others), but *anti*-natural. Not to say that God is "against" nature in an emotional sense, but God is a *correlate* to the world. Where there is social power or natural force, God is the space of possibility that cannot be expressed or defined within the dominant pattern. God is the restlessness or desire that underlies all stability.

The absent Christ serves as a corrective to two theological tendencies: the tendency to locate divine authority outside of the world, and the tendency to locate God within the world. Like all theological images, these tendencies shape the way we think about ourselves in relation to our communities and environment.

The two impulses more or less correspond to the conservative and liberal mindsets that are now, at least in the United States, more distinct and polarized than ever. It is not impossible to be an environmentalist and hold a supernaturalist theology, but supernaturalism tends to downplay the status of the natural world, because divine authority is kept distinct from the world.

Similarly, it is not impossible for an evangelical to hold a cosmopolitan orientation to politics, but here again a supernaturalist theology tends to support the idea of a national sovereign who exists above and apart from the legal framework. On the other hand, a naturalist orientation tends to have its own blind spots: an overly romantic view of nature or a naïve trust in the universality of Western ideals or in the consensus of any particular community.

The difference in the theological images of presence (at least uncomplicated presence) and absence is the difference between justification and interrogation. Historically, divine presence functions as a symbol for the shoring up of a system or an identity. In the Eucharist, divine presence grounds personal identity. In political theology, it feeds national identity. In ecology, it produces an ahistorical or anthropocentric view of nature.

Divine absence, on the other hand, functions as a question rather than an argument. Absence is no less demanding for all that, perhaps more so. It requires of us a commitment to continuous examination and creativity with respect to personal, social and global identities. It requires a commitment to the "messianic," in Derrida's sense, as that which cannot be defined ahead of time.[1] Briefly, we can summarize how divine absence might work on each of these three levels of existence: self, community and world.

Self and Others

We are used to thinking of ourselves as discrete entities, with personalities that persist through time. Individual existence and autonomy is one of the most basic assumptions of Western metaphysics, and it pervades everything from our justice system to our fairy tales to medical diagnosis. The theological idea of presence helps us to express this fundamental individualism by, for instance, thinking of redemption in personal terms. In Western theology, this is grounded in sacramental theology, especially Protestant theology, in which God is radically available to every person regardless of their social environment, gifting us with an unassailable self-identity.

It is very different to think of our identity as emerging only in the absence of Christ, where one has to shift one's glance downward and outward to find that fundamental, sacred grounding. In fact, we are all complex messes, hopelessly and beautifully interwoven. We are made up of many pieces held together, more or less coherently, by the narratives that we and others use as shorthand. And these pieces are always shifting around, which makes the task of narration that much more difficult, but also allows openings for new themes, character shifts, and dramatic reversals. We are, as Levinas says, constituted first of all by our relation to others and especially to Others—to our relations that make up part of our conscious and domesticated selfhood and those that challenge us and force us to accept the limitations of our self-narrative. To identify Christ as absent is to ground our ultimate loyalty particularly in the latter.

Does this not assume a certain masculine over-identity? Are we presupposing that the basic problem is one of too much self-confidence, whereas the problem for women and other minority groups is that they have not been given the same right or opportunity to a strong conception of the self? Certainly the landscape of the self looks quite different depending on one's relationship to dominant cultures, and the theological experience would be completely opposite; insofar as one inhabits a space of Otherness with regard to social norms, one can embody that deconstructive movement of the absent Christ.

Liberation itself, however, already assumes a relational ontology where the self is radically dependent on social power structures. Otherwise it would make no sense to link activism for material social conditions to theological commitment. A relational self does not mean a weak self. Even for those who have thoroughly developed comfortable self-identities, divine absence is not primarily a call to "weaken" identity but to prod identity to evolve out of stagnation, whether one begins from a position of relative strength or weakness.

Community and State

The same implications apply to the communities to which we belong. It is impossible for communities to avoid constructing a collective identity. We narrate our social story just as we do our personal stories. And, just as personal identity has a theological underpinning, so social identity has a theological correlate: the idea of Christ's presence within the church. This idea, too, finds its way into the secular West in the form of democracy and liberalism. In itself, social identities are not bad or wrong, just as personal identity is not an evil in itself. Again, there is no way to avoid constructing identities. The problem lies in the assumption that it is social identities that mediate the sacred.

In the context of churches, the idea of divine presence manifests itself in an overemphasis on unity and consensus. There is the assumption, spoken or unspoken, that the wisdom of the group is identical to the voice of God. Sometimes the word *discernment* is used (or abused) to distinguish a deliberation that is supposed to carry this kind of weight. Certainly decisions made with a wide variety of inputs are often better, easier to justify, and tend to result in more lasting change. Consensus is an improvement over hierarchical models of decision-making. But consensus has its limits. It is based on the knowledge, experiences, and biases of the participants. It may suppress ideas that run against the majority view or that would introduce radically new understandings. In short, it can sometimes reinforce the lowest common denominator for any given discussion. The limits of consensus represent the limits of social identity.

In a theology of absence, then, consensus is the name for the god-forsakenness of the community. The work of consensus can still be quite valuable, but the point is not to discover God's presence within that consensus. Rather, consensus outlines what is irrelevant to the community. It marks the frontiers of Christ's absence. For example, in a church that has discerned that it wants to affirm LGBTQ individuals and experiences as a legitimate part of communal life (and assuming that this is a genuine consensus among the participants), LGBTQ inclusion is not the place where Christ will appear to the community. Christ will be manifested, likely in ways that no one could predict, in the more difficult work of interpreting or implementing gender inclusivity, or perhaps in some completely unrelated issue that supplants sexuality as a major issue of confusion or concern for the community.

As a rule of thumb, Christ is always located at the edges of a community, instead of within. However, in some cases, just as with personal identity, a marginalized community may have social "edges" folded into its social identity, which might allow that community's consensus to embody Christ in certain respects vis-à-vis the broader social landscape.

But any community has its own core, which is visible, comfortable, and mundane—and beyond whose frontiers lies the invisible, unmapped, and unsettling Christ.

The concept of divine presence in the community also contributes to the confusion generated around the ideals of unity and tolerance. I hear for instance, much talk in both the church and in secular democracies about the necessity of being welcoming or inclusive to everyone, regardless of their political orientation, sexuality, theological beliefs, class, nationality, etc. This is an admirable sentiment, and it usually comes out of a desire to be responsive to minority groups. The confusion comes when it becomes apparent that there are mutually exclusive elements in a population. One cannot be inclusive both of a nativist and an immigrant, or a slumlord and a low-income family—in fact, the very attempt to do so erodes the possibility of real inclusion. Still, the idea of tolerance is strong enough that it becomes an argument for moderating the reforming energy of the community with the idea that fewer people will be offended. This is fundamentally a topological misunderstanding: it assumes that the community can and should occupy an infinite space.

It is interesting to look at the stories of Jesus in the Gospels, where he does not actually present a particularly welcoming or tolerant character. Certainly he is extraordinarily gracious to some groups (the sick, poor, children, women), but he also pronounces clear, perhaps even overly sharp judgments against others. Consider Matthew 23, where he says the scribes and Pharisees are vipers going to hell and, moreover, that they are guilty of all blood that has been spilled in human history.

The task of the church, then, is not necessarily to welcome everyone but to be cognizant of social power and therefore of the directional demand of Christ. The church, like any other community, occupies a finite space shaped by relational identities. It can make decisions about how to reshape that space, but the fundamental relationship between the communal space and the divine outside does not change. The question is not, how can we become unified or how can we incorporate all people into the community but who we will be given the challenge posed by the absent Christ.

The decentering work of the absent Christ has one final implication for our thinking about church and community. That is, there is no strict separation in the status of the church and other communities, including political or secular communities. Since all communities are locations of identity, they all constitute absences that are vulnerable to divine inbreaking. The church has no special dispensation to be the carrier of Christ to the world. One would hope, but this would have to be empirically tested, that the church would be more likely to attend to its limits, to maintain an attitude of welcome to the absence around its identity, and therefore to be more flexible and swift in its response to marginalized peoples. In reality, churches fall short of this ideal, perhaps even more so than secular communities in regards to some issues. In short, churches, as well as civic communities of whatever scale, may claim to mediate divine authority only insofar as they prove to be moving toward liberation, and not by virtue of an identity that can be claimed once and for all.[2]

It is in respect to its implications for ecclesiology that one might question the subtitle of this book as an "Anabaptist theology." Indeed, it should already be clear that this is not meant to be a recapitulation of sixteenth-century Anabaptist thinking. Although I see some deep structural similarities between, for instance, Hubmaier's Eucharist, Marx, and liberation theology, it would be completely anachronistic to claim that Hubmaier would embrace this theology or that the symbol of the absent Christ is the only legitimate line that can be extrapolated from that period. There are departures from orthodox theology here that would certainly perturb many contemporary Mennonites, and others would seek inspiration in different biblical texts or social contexts.

Still, the basic elements of this theology constitute, I believe, a faithful rearticulation of the Mennonite theological tradition. For one, I am deeply cognizant of the social context out of which Anabaptist theology began, a period in which people began questioning the right of political and ecclesial leaders to appropriate natural resources, oppress the poor, and use the church as a tool for maintaining national security. In the context of the twenty-first century, it makes sense to use the language of liberation and deconstruction to express this tradition. I also affirm the basic insights that the early Anabaptists had about the responsibility of the church to embody right relationships, the correlation of divine presence or absence with material relations, and the suspicion of national claims to divine authority. In all of these ways, the arguments above present a very traditional articulation of Mennonite theology.

Perhaps the most important contribution that the theology of the absent Christ makes to Mennonite theology is its reconsideration of the idea of the church as a divinely ordained community, "without spot or wrinkle." This is indeed a far cry from sixteenth-century ecclesiology, where some Anabaptists believed that it was truly possible, if only they could separate themselves from the rest of society, to create a perfectly faithful church. It is only too obvious that churches, like any other forms of community, are indeed spotted and wrinkly. In a context where we encounter "an institutional clergy structure and practice that protects the clergy and church institutions at the expense of the laity" (Ruth Krall's definition of clericalism),[3] it seems appropriate to draw on the anti-clerical history of Anabaptism, even if it is to be wielded against the tendency toward over-optimism that characterizes traditional Anabaptist ecclesiology.

Humans and Nature

Finally, the same logic that the absent Christ brings to social issues might apply metaphysically: i.e., there is no strict separation between human communities and the natural world. Certainly, humans have characteristics that are not present or less present in other species. In particular, when we shift from thinking about human society to the rest of the natural world, we should not think of the absent Christ as presenting a moral demand in the same way. But the basic theological framework presented here does have implications for how we think about the physical world in general. To put it briefly, the world is a relational landscape defined by the myriad interactions between creatures. It is a construction emerging from historical, social behavior characterized by power and creativity, and is therefore radically contingent on those relationships.

Humans, of course, are an increasingly disruptive factor in our earthly landscape. In fact, because of the level of disruption in the past two centuries, it is now possible to think about the earth itself as needing liberation from us. In that sense, God could be associated with the earth, and seen as making a divine demand upon human societies. But this kind of identification of God and earth should be carefully separated from the idea that God is identical with the natural order as something static or ahistorical. Conservation, preservation, or sustainability is not the goal per se; in fact, none of those concepts are particularly "natural" if you look at the long arm of physical or biological history. "Nature" in the abstract makes no demand upon us, only actual relations in a historical trajectory. But the dynamism and contingency of nature do not mean that humans have no responsibility—precisely the opposite. It is because our decisions have the potential to radically alter ecosystems and natural patterns that we must think very carefully about what kind of ecological future we are constructing for ourselves and the rest of the earth.

NOTES

Introduction

1. Rachel Waltner Goossen, "'Defanging the Beast': Mennonite Responses to John Howard Yoder's Sexual Abuse," *Mennonite Quarterly Review* 89, no. 1 (2015): 7-80.

2. Ruth Krall, *The Elephant in God's Living Room*, vol. 3 (n.p., 2013), https://ruthkrall.com/downloadable-books/volume-three-the-mennonite-church-and-john-howard-yoder-collected-essays/.

3. Paraphrased from Bava Metzia 59a-b. See https://www.sefaria.org/Bava_Metzia.59a.12.

4. "Representations of Jesus holding a magic wand gradually disappear after the beginning of the fifth century, when the wand is sometimes transformed to a cross, or dropped altogether. . . . [T]he wand was an attribute that was gradually phased out—perhaps because viewers were more and more removed from a time when competing with the other gods or wonderworking was necessary. By the end of the fifth century the contest was over." Robin Margaret Jensen, *Understanding Early Christian Art* (London; New York: Routledge, 2013), 124.

5. Gregory of Nyssa, *The Life of Moses* (Mahwah, N.J.: Paulist Press, 1978), 80-81.

6. I think specifically of John Howard Yoder's emphasis on consensus as a mark of truth, in conjunction with the complicity of church leaders to cover up his abuse of countless women.

Chapter One

1. Quoted in Daniel Alan Smith, *Revisiting the Empty Tomb: The Early History of Easter* (Minneapolis: Fortress Press, 2010), 177.

2. See, for example, Bart D. Ehrman, *Jesus: Apocalyptic Prophet of the New Millennium* (Oxford: Oxford University Press, 1999).

3. The use of Psalm 18 in chapter titles is a gesture toward these themes.

4. See Richard Elliott Friedman, *The Hidden Face of God* (Harper Collins, 1996).

5. "Thus the appearance tradition finally enters—*literally*—the empty and enticingly suggestive space of the disappearance tradition when the rising Jesus appeared in the tomb and on his way out. . . . This paradoxical pattern of attempted subordination and persisting influence is seen in the narrative, apologetic, and hagiographical deployments of the empty tomb story well beyond the second century." Smith, *Revisiting the Empty Tomb*, 182.

6. "I would suggest that the canon and norm for evaluating biblical traditions and their subsequent interpretations cannot be derived from the Bible or the biblical process of learning within ideologies, but can only be formulated within the struggle for the liberation of women and all oppressed people. The canon and evaluative norm cannot be 'universal,' but must be specific and derived from a particular experience of oppression and liberation." Elisabeth Schüssler Fiorenza, *Bread Not Stone: The Challenge of Feminist Biblical Interpretation* (Beacon Press, 1995), 60. See also Smith, *Revisiting the Empty Tomb*, 184: "[The disappearance traditions] never conveyed ideas about a private vindication that had no meaning beyond what it meant for Jesus—they had a community focus, and they arose and found narrative expression, elaboration, and deployment in communities that sought to describe how life should be in light of God's vindication of Jesus."

7. Brian DuWayne Robinette, *Grammars of Resurrection: A Christian Theology of Presence and Absence* (New York: Crossroad Pub. Co, 2009).

8. See, for example, Smith, *Revisiting the Empty Tomb*. or Elisabeth Schüssler Fiorenza, *Jesus: Miriam's Child, Sophia's Prophet* (New York: Continuum, 1995).

9. Schüssler Fiorenza, *Jesus: Miriam's Child, Sophia's Prophet*, 122.

10. Schüssler Fiorenza, 126.

11. Sarah Coakley, *Powers and Submissions: Spirituality, Philosophy, and Gender* (Oxford; Malden, Mass.: Blackwell Publishers, 2002), 11.

12. Coakley, 7-8.

13. John Howard Yoder's interpretation of kenosis is very similar to Coakley's here. "[Jesus'] way to be the anointed one was to be not the ruler but the servant—to empty himself. His way to be godlike was human-like. Jesus made that choice not once but over and over. He refused in the desert to be a Che Guevara or a George Washington. Instead, he held people's children, in an age before Pampers. He washed people's dirty feet. He healed their hemorrhages. He forgave their sins. . . . He remained the servant all the way to his death." John Howard Yoder, *He Came Preaching Peace* (Scottdale, Pa.: Herald Press, 1985), 89-95. See also Yoder's extended analysis of Philippians 2: John Howard Yoder, *Preface to Theology: Christology and Theological Method* (Grand Rapids, Mich.: Brazos Press, 2002), 80-87. Gerald Mast also makes this connection between Coakley and Yoder. See Gerald Mast, "Pacifism as a Way of Knowing," in *John Howard Yoder: Radical Theologian*, ed. J.

Denny Weaver (Eugene, Ore.: Cascade Books, 2014), 230-235.

14. Coakley, *Powers and Submissions*, 10. Coakley points out that this metaphysical claim is similar to Rosemary Radford Ruether's interpretation of kenosis as a divine repudiation of patriarchy. Rosemary Radford Ruether, *Sexism and God-Talk: Toward a Feminist Theology* (Boston: Beacon Press, 1983), 137-138.

15. "We are very far from the cross of Christ just being an event of the past, or the prerequisite of resurrection, or Jesus' answer to the question of his mission. The cross is now our whole attitude in the world. It is the fact that Jew and Gentile relate as sisters and brothers; that is what they would have been persecuted for. . . . So again, it is the concept of solidarity." Yoder, *Preface to Theology*, 104-105. This quote comes in the context of Yoder's discussion of the various ways that early Christian writers made connections between their audience and Jesus' message. Thus this quote represents Yoder's interpretation of Paul's concept of kenosis, not necessarily Yoder's personal view. At the same time, he does seem to imply that Paul's idea of solidarity is still relevant to us as we think about our own connections to the story of Jesus.

16. Juan Marin, "A Lukan Kenosis? Luke's Concept of Truth as an Ethics of Service," *Journal of Philosophy and Scripture* 6, no. 1 (2009): 4.

17. Marin, 5.

18. Marin, 7.

19. "Kenosis, rather, involves the dissolution of metaphysical absolutes, the reduction of metaphysical violence, the liberation of multiple voices. Rather than representing the final truth that supersedes and overcomes the partial truth of other myths, incarnation, kenotically understood, is secularization, the liberation of hermeneutical plurality." Marta Marta Frascati-Lochhead, *Kenosis and Feminist Theology: The Challenge of Gianni Vattimo* (Albany, N.Y.: State University of New York Press, 1998), 161-162.

20. "Christianity begins with a disappearance. To be sure, the New Testament witnesses to an 'appearance'. . . . But the appearances of Jesus also imply a dis-appearance, namely the withdrawal of a body. In Mark, the women approach the tomb of the crucified Jesus only to be startled. Expecting to see and anoint a body, what they witnessed instead was a shocking absence. The tomb was empty. . . . They were then given instructions to go to Galilee to tell the disciples what they saw, which was literally no-thing. There, among the disciples *in community*, they would encounter the risen Jesus who has gone before them." Robinette, *Grammars of Resurrection*, 25.

21. One could compare this, again, to Gregory of Nyssa's concept of divine darkness as "dark light" or "luminous darkness." Gregory of Nyssa, *The Life of Moses*, 80-81.

22. Quoted in Jane M.F. Heath, "Absent Presences of Paul and Christ: Enargeia in 1 Thessalonians 1-3," *Journal for the Study of the New Testament* 32, no. 1 (2009): 9.

23. Heinrich F. Plett, *Enargeia in Classical Antiquity and the Early Modern Age: The Aesthetics of Evidence* (Leiden: Brill, 2012), 8.

24. Plett, 9.

25. Ruth Webb, *Ekphrasis, Imagination and Persuasion in Ancient Rhetorical Rheory and Practice* (Farnham, Surrey; Burlington, Vt.: Ashgate, 2009), 195.

26. Philip Hardie, *Ovid's Poetics of Illusion* (Cambridge; New York: Cambridge University Press, 2002), 11.

27. Heath, "Absent Presences of Paul and Christ," 22.

28. Heath, 26.

29. Luke 1:1-4 (NRSV): "Since many have undertaken to set down an orderly account of the events that have been fulfilled among us, just as they were handed on to us by those who from the beginning were eyewitnesses and servants of the word, I too decided, after investigating everything carefully from the very first, to write an orderly account for you, most excellent Theophilus, so that you may know the truth concerning the things about which you have been instructed."

30. Schüssler Fiorenza, *Jesus: Miriam's Child, Sophia's Prophet*, 128.

31. "For Lévinas, God initially 'comes to the idea' or 'falls into meaning' in the ethical relation where I am exposed to the infinite claims made on me by the other. The trace of God is put into me as I say 'Here I am' in response to the command constituted by the transcendence and destitution of the other, before being for myself." Marie L. Baird, "Revisioning Christian Theology in Light of Emmanuel Levinas's Ethics of Responsibility," *Journal of Ecumenical Studies* 36, no. 3-4 (1999): 349.

32. Matt. 28:6; Mark 16:6; Luke 24:5.

Chapter Two

1. Gregory of Nyssa, *The Life of Moses*.

2. Julian of Norwich, *Revelations of Divine Love*, trans. Frances Beer (Cambridge: D. S. Brewer, 1998), 37.

3. "While much mystical language about absence is indeed existentially powerful and poetically stirring, for the Christian mystic the consciousness of divine absence is always related to consciousness of divine presence." Julia A. Lamm, "A Guide to Christian Mysticism," in *The Wiley-Blackwell Companion to Christian Mysticism* (Hoboken, N.J.: John Wiley & Sons, 2017), 4.

4. The term is from Michael Allen Gillespie, *The Theological Origins of Modernity* (Chicago: University Of Chicago Press, 2009). Note that Ockham drew on many other theologians before him who had articulated similar principles. But Ockham's was the clearest exposition of what would later be called nominalism.

5. Gillespie, 24-25.

6. "Anticlericalism prior to the Reformation stressed the need for ecclesiastical reform, since contemporaries had not given up hope for a thoroughgoing reform of the clerical hierarchy. This kind of anticlericalism critiqued the gradualistic approach from within the system. . . . Anticlericalism at the time of the Reformation, by contrast, sought to do away with the clerical estate altogether since it was no longer needed as a mediator between God and human beings." Hans-Jürgen Goertz, "Karlstadt, Muntzer and the Reformation of the Commoners, 1521-1525," in *A Companion to Anabaptism and Spiritualism, 1521-1700*, ed. John Roth and James

Stayer (Leiden: Brill, 2007), 3.

7. "Anticlericalism is a collective term, gaining currency in the nineteenth century as a one-sided negative designation. Properly understood, it describes attitudes and forms of behavior which in late medieval and early modern Europe engendered literary, political or physical action against what were perceived as unjust privileges constituting the legal, political, economic, sexual, sacred or social power of the clergy. Significantly different according to place, time and social background, anticlericalism could focus on papal, episcopal, sacerdotal, monastic, ministerial or intellectual power structures." Peter A. Dykema and Heiko Augustinus Oberman, eds., *Anticlericalism in Late Medieval and Early Modern Europe* (Leiden: Brill, 1993), x. Hans-Jürgen Goertz claims that anticlericalism was the one commonality shared by all the reforming groups, each of whom moderated this anticlericalism to different degrees. Goertz, "Karlstadt, Muntzer and the Reformation of the Commoners," 4.

8. "Based on these insights, we might see reformation anticlericalism as part of the mentality of a revolutionary situation, not as a reasoned response to escalating clerical corruption. The explanation focuses less on inherent, religious characteristics of the clergy as a social group than on their relationships to the broader distinctions between wealth and poverty, power and impotence, and respectability and despicability." Thomas A. Brady Jr., "'You Hate Us Priests': Anticlericalism, Communalism, and the Control of Women at Strasbourg in the Age of the Reformation," in *Anticlericalism in Late Medieval and Early Modern Europe*, ed. Peter A. Dykema and Heiko Augustinus Oberman (Leiden: Brill, 1993), 170.

9. See James Stayer's description of various historiographical frameworks for understanding Anabaptism. Scholars have, at different times, distinguished Anabaptists based on basic religious themes—evangelical, rational, revolutionary, radical spiritualist, sacramental spiritualist, noetic spiritualist, anti-Trinitarian, etc.—or by regional variations—Swiss/South German, Dutch, Moravian, South German/Austrian, Zurich, Bohemian, Silesian. James Stayer, "Introduction," in *A Companion to Anabaptism and Spiritualism, 1521-1700* (Leiden: Brill, 2007), xxiii-xxiv.

10. "Within this framework, the affirmation of God as hidden, as the Abiding Mystery immediately present to human self-transcendence, does not negate but sublates the positive biblical and creedal affirmations of faith. In Rahner's language, Christian faith is a mediated immediacy: as Abiding Mystery, God not simply the Unknown, but the Known Unknown, and the affirmative moment of Christian faith, reflectively described according to the procedures of an *analogia entis* or an *analogia fidei*, remains necessary, albeit qualified, as itself penultimate in comparison with the reality of God." Joseph A. Colombo, "God as Hidden, God as Manifest: 'Who Is the Subject of Salvation in History in Liberation Theology?,'" *The Journal of Religion* 71, no. 1 (1991): 21.

11. Alister E. McGrath, *Luther's Theology of the Cross: Martin Luther's Theological Breakthrough* (Oxford: Blackwell, 1985), 165.

12. Colombo, "God as Hidden, God as Manifest," 21-22; McGrath, *Luther's*

Theology of the Cross, 165.

13. John D. Rempel, *The Lord's Supper in Anabaptism: A Study in the Christology of Balthasar Hubmaier, Pilgram Marpeck, and Dirk Philips* (Waterloo, Ont.; Scottdale, Pa.: Herald Press, 1993), 51.

14. Rob Sorensen, *Martin Luther and the German Reformation* (London: Anthem, 2016), 55.

15. "Calvin, following Zwingli, suggested that the whole universe is full of the divinity of Christ but his human body is in heaven. . . . Therefore, Christ cannot be physically present in the eucharist. However, it is true that Christ is always with his children. In the eucharist, the body of Christ is taken by participants and his blood is absorbed in their body and spirit. At this point, Calvin agrees with Luther. In understanding Calvin's eucharistic theology, the key is the role of the Holy Spirit in the eucharist. By the secret power of the Holy Spirit, the body of Christ in heaven is given to the partakers in the eucharist." Eojin Lee, *Theology of the Open Table* (Eugene, Ore.: Wipf and Stock Publishers, 2016), 131.

16. Quoted in Carrie Euler, "Huldrych Zwingli and Heinrich Bullinger," in *A Companion to the Eucharist in the Reformation,* ed. Lee Palmer Wandel (Leiden: Brill, 2014), 64.

17. Here I follow MacGregor's reading of Hubmaier rather than Rempel's. See Kirk R. MacGregor, *A Central European Synthesis of Radical and Magisterial Reform: The Sacramental Theology of Balthasar Hubmaier* (Lanham, Md.: University Press of America, 2006).

18. "Unlike Zwingli and the Anabaptists, who refer to the church as the body of Christ in a symbolic sense, Hubmaier employs theologically precise linguistic handles, such as the noun *Wesen* (nature or essence) and the adjective *wesentlich* (essentially or substantially), to argue that an ontological shift followed the consumption of the respective elements. Upon this consumption, the members of the visible church became the res, the physical body and blood of Christ, to which the signa of bread and wine were pointing." MacGregor, 195.

19. "To explain what this formula means, Hubmaier appeals to his Anselmian dichotomy between the definitive and repletive presence of Christ's physical body. At the respective moments that believers, in the act of remembrance, eat the bread and drink the wine, Christ, whose humanity is definitively present . . . in heaven, fills the believers with the repletive presence . . . of his body and blood in a special sacramental way." MacGregor, 194.

20. Balthasar Hubmaier, "Several Theses Concerning the Mass," in *Balthasar Hubmaier, Theologian of Anabaptism,* trans. H. Wayne Pipkin and John Howard Yoder (Scottdale, Pa.: Herald Press, 1989), 75.

21. "For he is with [the church] himself by his grace until the end of the world . . . although bodily he has ascended into heaven where he sits at the right hand of his heavenly Father there in heaven. . . . He has a particular place 'in heaven, in heaven' and not everywhere, as deity is omnipresent. Yea, neither in the bread nor in the wine nor in other creatures." Balthasar Hubmaier, "On the Christian Ban," in *Balthasar*

Hubmaier, Theologian of Anabaptism, trans. H. Wayne Pipkin and John Howard Yoder (Scottdale, Pa.: Herald Press, 1989), 415.

22. John Rempel sees the emphasis on Christ's absence as "severing the breaking of bread from communion with Christ." Rempel, *The Lord's Supper in Anabaptism*, 89. I would suggest the opposite: that Christ's bodily absence is actually what allows for a true distinction and therefore true communion between Christ and church. See also MacGregor's criticism of Rempel: "These criticisms, however, are only as strong as the presupposition on which they are based, i.e., that for Hubmaier, the elements constitute the only possible bearers of the real presence. But if Hubmaier regarded something besides the elements as bearing the real presence, then these criticisms fall to the ground. We shall see that this is, in fact, the situation, as Hubmaier regarded the human participants themselves as bearing the real presence. However, Hubmaier stressed that humans could only bear the real presence through receiving the Eucharist. Hence there exists no other means for humanity to bear the real presence save for the sacramental acts of communally eating the bread and drinking the wine, due to Christ's institution and divine empowerment of the Eucharist for that specific purpose. As a result, Hubmaier's case proves to be quite coherent, and the aforementioned dissonance is easily resolved." Kirk R. MacGregor, "The Eucharistic Theology and Ethics of Balthasar Hubmaier," *Harvard Theological Review* 105, no. 2 (2012): 229.

23. MacGregor, *A Central European Synthesis*, 198.

24. Hubmaier, "Several Theses Concerning the Mass," 76.

25. "[T]here are two kinds of knowledge; one is of faith, which we derive from the word, though the thing itself does not appear; the other is of experience, when God adds accomplishment to the promise and proves that he has not spoken in vain." Quoted in Charles Partee, *Calvin and Classical Philosophy* (Louisville, Ky.: Westminster John Knox Press, 2005), 39-40.

26. See Gillespie, *The Theological Origins of Modernity*. for an account of the effect of nominalism on the Enlightenment and the modern world.

27. John Howard Yoder wrote extensively on the topic of foundationalism and the Anabaptist/Mennonite alternative to foundationalism, and it has continued to be a strong enough theme in Mennonite theology to justify a place on David Cramer's list of characteristics of any future Mennonite theologies: David Cramer, "Mennonite Systematic Theology in Retrospect and Prospect," *Conrad Grebel Review* 31, no. 3 (Fall 2013): 255-273.

28. "The office of such a person shall be to read and exhort and teach, warn, admonish, or ban in the congregation, and properly to preside among the sisters and brothers in prayer, and in the breaking of the bread, and in all things to take care of the body of Christ." John Howard Yoder, ed., *The Schleitheim Confession* (Scottdale, Pa.: Herald Press, 1977), 13.

29. Hans-Jürgen Goertz, *The Anabaptists*, trans. Trevor Johnson (London: Routledge, 1996), 45.

30. Probably not the same group as the Swiss Anabaptists of the Schleitheim

Confession, but a rival Moravian group whose elder came from Switzerland. See Martin Rothkegel, "Pilgram Marpeck and the Fellows of the Covenant: The Short and Fragmentary History of the Rise and Decline of an Anabaptist Denominational Network," *Mennonite Quarterly Review* 85, no. 1 (2011): 34-36. and Werner O. Packull, *Hutterite Beginnings: Communitarian Experiments during the Reformation* (Baltimore, Md: Johns Hopkins University Press, 1995), 287-289.

31. Pilgram Marpeck, *The Writings of Pilgram Marpeck*, ed. William Klassen and Walter Klaassen (Kitchener, Ont.; Scottdale, Pa.: Herald Press, 1978), 448–50.

32. Thieleman J. van Braght, *The Bloody Theater, or, Martyrs Mirror*, trans. Joseph F. Sohm, 5th ed (Scottdale, Pa.: Herald Press, 1950), 741.

33. In some cases this is quite literal. Bulgarian iconographer Jivko Donkov depicts Luiken's etching of Willems. Available for purchase at http://www.found-goshen.com/anabaptist-icons/.

34. See Stephanie Krehbiel, "Staying Alive: How Martyrdom Made Me a Warrior," *Mennonite Life* 61, no. 4 (2006), http://archive.bethelks.edu/ml/issue/vol-61-no-4/.

Chapter Three

1. Emmanuel Lévinas, *Emmanuel Levinas: Basic Philosophical Writings* (Bloomington, Ind.: Indiana University Press, 1996), 29.

2. Wilfred Cantwell Smith, *The Meaning and End of Religion* (Minneapolis: Fortress Press, 1964), 20.

3. One major example is political sovereignty or authority. See chapter 5.

4. This should evoke echoes of liberation theology. For example: "I believe the christology of the cross described above helps us to find [Christ's body] in the crucified people and to see the saving mystery of the cross in them. Therefore we can say that the crucified people are Christ's crucified body in history. But the opposite is also true: the present-day crucified people allow us to know the crucified Christ better." Jon Sobrino, *Jesus the Liberator: A Historical-Theological Reading of Jesus of Nazareth*, trans. Paul Burns and Francis McDonagh (Maryknoll, N.Y.: Orbis Books, 1993), 264.

5. "The Other is not other with a relative alterity as are, in a comparison, even ultimate species, which mutually exclude one another but still have their place within the community of a genus—excluding one another by their definition, but calling for one another by this exclusion, across the community of their genus. The alterity of the Other does not depend on any quality that would distinguish him from me, for a distinction of this nature would precisely imply between us that community of genus which already nullifies alterity." Emmanuel Lévinas, *Totality and Infinity: An Essay on Exteriority*, trans. Alphonso Lingis (The Hague: M. Nijhoff Publishers, 1979), 194.

6. Nathan Widder, *Political Theory after Deleuze* (London: Continuum International Pub. Group, 2015), 12.

7. "The Other who can sovereignly say *no* to me is exposed to the point of the

sword or the bullet has touched the ventricles or auricles of his heart. In the contexture of the world he is a quasi-nothing. But he can oppose to me a struggle, that is, oppose to the force that strikes him not a force or resistance, but the very unforeseeableness of his reaction. He thus opposed to me not a greater force, an energy assessable and consequently presenting itself as though it were a part of a whole, but the very transcendence of his being by relation to that whole; not some superlative of power, but precisely the infinity of his transcendence. This infinity, stronger than murder, already resists us in his face, is his face, is the primordial *expression*, is the first word: 'you shall not commit murder.'" Lévinas, *Totality and Infinity*, 199.

8. "Something in the world forces us to think. This something is an object not of recognition but of a fundamental *encounter*. What is encountered may be Socrates, a temple or a demon. It may be grasped in a range of affective tones: wonder, love, hatred, suffering. In whichever tone, its primary characteristic is that it can only be sensed. In this sense it is opposed to recognition." Gilles Deleuze, *Difference and Repetition*, trans. Paul Patton, Revised ed. (New York: Columbia University Press, 1995), 139.

9. Immanuel Kant, *Critique of Judgement*, ed. Nicholas Walker, trans. James Creed Meredith (Oxford: Oxford University Press, 2009), 75-76.

10. "The sublime is that, the mere capacity of thinking which evidences a faculty of mind transcending every standard of the senses." Kant, 81.

11. "Idealism completely carried out reduces all ethics to politics. The Other and the I function as elements of an ideal calculus, receive from this calculus their real being, and approach one another under the dominion of ideal necessities which traverse them from all sides. They pay the role of moments in a system, and not that of origin." Lévinas, *Totality and Infinity*, 216.

12. "What, then, can we conclude about the meaning of God's love in a racist society? Using blackness as the point of departure, black theology believes that God's love of humankind is revealed in God's willingness to become black. God's love is incomprehensible apart from blackness. This means that to love blacks God takes on black oppressed existence, becoming one of us. God is black because God loves us; and God loves us because we are black." James H. Cone, *A Black Theology of Liberation*, 20th anniversary ed. (Maryknoll, N.Y.: Orbis Books, 1990), 73.

13. For example, Marx believes that the distinction between the profits based on interest and production allows owners of production to consider themselves merely as highly paid workers rather than exploiters of workers. "Since the estranged character of capital, its antithesis to labor, is shifted outside the actual process of exploitation, i.e. into interest-bearing capital, this process of exploitation itself appears as simply a labour process, in which the functioning capitalist simply performs different work from that of the workers. The labour of exploiting is just as much labour as the labour that is exploited." Karl Marx, *Capital: Volume 3*, trans. David Fernbach (London; New York: Penguin Classics, 1992), 506.

14. Widder, *Political Theory after Deleuze*, 52-53.

15. Quoted in Ada María Isasi-Díaz, *En La Lucha (In the Struggle): A Hispanic*

Women's Liberation Theology (Minneapolis: Fortress Press, 1993), 75.

16. Gilles Deleuze and Félix Guattari, *A Thousand Plateaus: Capitalism and Schizophrenia* (London: Continuum, 2004), 320.

Chapter Four

1. Alfred North Whitehead, *Process and Reality*, Corrected ed (New York: Free Press, 1978), 351.

2. "Scholastic metaphysics understood God as the highest being and creation as a rational order of beings stretching up to God. From the nominalist perspective, however, such an order is untenable not only because each being is radically individual but also and perhaps more importantly because God himself is not a being in the same sense as all created beings." Gillespie, *The Theological Origins of Modernity*, 35.

3. Maxwell Kennel traces the historical antipathy between Mennonites and metaphysics, as well as the more recent engagement of Mennonites with philosophy, metaphysics and postmodernity. Maxwell Kennel, "Mennonite Metaphysics? Exploring the Philosophical Aspects of Mennonite Theology from Pacifist Epistemology to Ontological Peace," *Mennonite Quarterly Review* 91, no. 3 (2017): 403-421.

4. See Jean-François Lyotard's assertion that narratives are potentially the most violent type of discourse. *The Differend: Phrases in Dispute* (Minneapolis: University of Minnesota Press, 1988), 151.

5. See Elaine Enn's research on Mennonites in the Ukraine: "I learned that Nogai and Cossack peoples, the traditional inhabitants of the Ukrainian steppes, had been forcibly removed by Catherine the Great just prior to my ancestors arriving from Prussia in the 1780s. Here is a case of complex historical truth: Mennonite emigrants from one part of Europe end up displacing indigenous people in another part of Europe. A people desiring only religious freedom were used in a wider imperial scheme to colonize marginal lands. And it gets even more complicated. The Russian Mennonites who did make it out in the 1920s (including my grandparents) came as refugees to the Canadian prairies. They were given or bought land in areas that had recently been taken from Cree tribes by the Canadian government. Here again, Mennonite victims in one part of the world, trying only to survive, helped disenfranchise First Nations people half a world away." Elaine Enns, "Pilgrimage to the Ukraine: Revisioning History through Restorative Justice," Bartimaeus Cooperative Ministries, accessed January 10, 2015, http://www.bcm-net.org/pilgrimage-to-the-ukraine-revisioning-history-through-restorative-justice-elaine-enns.

6. Millard Lind, for example, believes that biblical nonviolence is grounded in the idea that Yahweh takes responsibility for judgment and vengeance on evildoers. Only because of God's violence is the church able to give up the need to use violence. *Yahweh Is a Warrior: The Theology of Warfare in Ancient Israel* (Scottdale, Pa.: Herald Press, 1980). J. Denny Weaver argues that Lind's view, though written in defense of pacifism, still champions violence as an ultimate solution for conflict. "Although Lind's account softens the image of a God who kills by having the deaths occur through natural occurrences, ultimately it is still God who is depicted as the origin of

the forces of nature that kill." J. Denny Weaver, *The Nonviolent God* (Grand Rapids, Mich.: Eerdmans, 2013), 110.

7. "For must not historical action—to be truly responsible—have some ontological and dogmatic basis? Is the biblical confession that 'Jesus is Lord' itself not implicitly a metaphysical and ontological statement of some kind?" A. James Reimer, *Mennonites and Classical Theology: Dogmatic Foundations for Christian Ethics* (Kitchener, Ont.: Pandora Press, 2001), 202.

8. Microhistory was first developed by Italian historians of the 1970s (Carlo Ginzburg, Giovanni Levi), and reached the height of its popularity in the 1990s. It continues to be influential, especially since the founding of the Center for Microhistorical Research in Reykjavik. Sigurður Gylfi Magnússon and István M. Szijártó, eds., *What Is Microhistory?* (Routledge, 2013), 5-6.

9. Magnússon and Szijártó, 5.

10. Georg G. Iggers, *Historiography in the Twentieth Century: From Scientific Objectivity to the Postmodern Challenge* (Middletown, Conn.: Wesleyan University Press, 2005), 103.

11. Iggers' definition of microhistory is "the concentration on an individual in a given locality and the attempt to stress the difference of this very local setting from a larger norm." Iggers, 111.

12. This term can also be used to describe metaphysics that ground complexity in the small. Whitehead's metaphysics has been called a "micrometaphysics" in this sense, but I am using the term here in a different way. See Eric Alliez, *The Signature of the World, or, What Is Deleuze and Guattari's Philosophy?* (London; New York: Continuum, 2004), 57.

13. Even Reimer acknowledges the possibility of multiple Anabaptist theologies, though he believes there are fairly rigid categories upon which all Mennonite theologies should build, namely the classic doctrine of the Trinity. "Because of the heterogenous and polygenetic nature of sixteenth-century Anabaptism and of 450 years of Mennonitism, and especially in light of the multiplicity of ethnic, cultural and religious emphases in the contemporary Mennonite church, it seems perfectly in order that we would encourage a variety of comprehensively conceived Anabaptist-Mennonite systematic theologies." Reimer, *Mennonites and Classical Theology*, 207-208.

14. Thomas Finger and A. James Reimer, for example, attempt to solve the problem of foundationalism by positing an eschatological universal, which can only break into history from the future, and therefore cannot be proven true or discovered rationally. As Finger says "Here universal truth . . . is present as a goal towards which people strive from the vantage-point of their own particularity. Theologically, universal truth is an eschatological reality. It is 'not yet' fully present—it is something that we will fully know and experience only at the End. Yet it is 'already' present–something which we grasp partially and which draws us further on." Thomas N. Finger, "Appropriating Other Traditions While Remaining Anabaptist," *Conrad Grebel Review* 17, no. 2 (1999): 52-68.

15. Technically, Whitehead defines "actual occasion" as a temporal event, which

excludes God. God is therefore an actual entity but not an actual occasion. "Actual event" and "actual entity" can be used synonymously, though "actual event" suggests the temporal nature of reality while "actual entity" suggests the spatial. See Gregory Nixon, "Whitehead and the Elusive Present: Process Philosophy's Creative Core," *Journal of Consciousness Exploration & Research* 1, no. 5 (2010): 629.

16. Whitehead, *Process and Reality*, 343.

17. Whitehead, 342.

18. "From this point of view, [God] is the principle of concretion—the principle whereby there is initiated a definite outcome from a situation otherwise riddled with ambiguity." Whitehead, 345.

19. Whitehead, 348.

20. See also Marjorie Suchocki, *The End of Evil: Process Eschatology in Historical Context* (Albany, N.Y.: State University of New York Press, 1988).

21. Whitehead, *Process and Reality*, 347.

22. Whitehead, 350-351.

23. Whitehead, 24.

24. "By reason of the actuality of this primordial valuation of pure potentials, each eternal object has a definite, effective relevance to each concrescent process. Apart from such orderings, there would be a complete disjunction of eternal objects unrealized in the temporal world. Novelty would be meaningless, and inconceivable." Whitehead, 40.

25. John B. Cobb and David Ray Griffin, *Process Theology: An Introductory Exposition* (Philadelphia: Westminster Press, 1976), 28.

26. Lewis S. Ford, *Transforming Process Theism* (Albany, N.Y.: State University of New York Press, 2000), 256.

27. Ford, 257.

28. Ford, 258.

29. Ford, 258.

30. Catherine Keller, "The Mystery of the Insoluble Evil: Violence and Evil in Marjorie Suchocki," in *World Without End: Christian Eschatology from a Process Perspective*, ed. Joseph A. Bracken (Grand Rapids, Mich.: Eerdmans, 2005), 63.

31. Catherine Keller, *Face of the Deep: A Theology of Becoming* (London: Routledge, 2003), 219.

32. Keller, 219.

33. Keller, 233.

34. Keller, 232.

35. Keller, 233.

36. "[O]ur intent ought not to be to develop a 'Mennonite' or 'Believers Church' theology as though this were an enterprise distinct from the ecumenical-Christian theological task. We are first and foremost Christians engaged in Christian theological reflection." Reimer, *Mennonites and Classical Theology*, 233.

37. Reimer, 178.

38. For one example, see Andrew P. Klager, "Balthasar Hubmaier's Use of the

Church Fathers: Availability, Access and Interaction," *Mennonite Quarterly Review* 84, no. 1 (2010).

39. Reimer, *Mennonites and Classical Theology*, 181.

40. Here I am drawing on both Keller and Yoder: Keller, *Face of the Deep*, 232-33. "What authorizes [reconciliation] in the Gospel account is the presence of the Spirit of Christ." John Howard Yoder, *For the Nations: Essays Evangelical and Public* (Grand Rapids, Mich.: Eerdmans, 1997), 30.

41. Reimer, *Mennonites and Classical Theology*, 243.

42. "This move to acknowledge the Powers within the church may be the most urgent course correction required of the radical theological vision associated with Yoder and with the Anabaptist Vision. As I write this, the failure of the broader historic Anabaptist movement to confront the sin of corrupted power within the church is increasingly visible, perhaps most strikingly among some traditional Mennonite communities where the virtues of humility and service have been so thoroughly cultivated." Gerald Mast, "Sin and Failure in Anabaptist Theology," in *John Howard Yoder: Radical Theologian*, ed. J. Denny Weaver (Eugene, Ore.: Cascade Books, 2014), 368.

43. Lyotard, *The Differend*. See also Justin Heinzekehr, "A Critique of Pure Justice: The Antinomy of John Howard Yoder," *Mennonite Life* 68, no. 1 (2014), http://archive.bethelks.edu/ml/issue/vol-68/article/a-critique-of-pure-justice-the-antinomy-of-john-ho/.

Chapter Five

1. Vegetius, *Epitome of Military Science*, trans. N. P. Milner (Liverpool: Liverpool University Press, 1996), 2.5 (pp 34-35).

2. See also William T. Cavanaugh, *The Myth of Religious Violence: Secular Ideology and the Roots of Modern Conflict* (New York: Oxford University Press, 2009).

3. For Barth, Christianity is the locus of "true religion" because it understands truth in terms of revelation and grace instead of religion in the usual sense. Karl Barth, *Church Dogmatics*, vol. 1.2 (Edinburgh: T. & T. Clark, 1936), 298.

4. Rene Girard, *Things Hidden Since the Foundation of the World*, trans. Stephen Bann and Michael Metter (Stanford, Calif.lif.: Stanford University Press, 1987).

5. Girard, 206.

6. Girard, 227-231.

7. "The author of the Epistle to the Hebrews would, of course, be the first to acknowledge that Christ was unjustly put to death. But his sacrificial reading takes little account of human responsibility for the death of Christ. The murderers are merely the instruments of divine will; it is hard to see how they could be found guilty." Girard, 231.

8. Girard, 196.

9. "The word 'sacrifice'—sacri-fice—means making sacred, producing the sacred." Girard, 226.

10. Girard, 231.

11. Girard, 216.

12. Girard, 53.

13. Girard, 66.

14. "What gives rise to the confusion, of course, is the habit of tracing structural analogies between the Passion and the sacrifices instituted by all other religions. . . . One can only escape these seductive analogies and detect the signs that point unequivocally to the opposition between the two forms of transcendence by realizing that the gospel text has achieved its anthropological fulfillment in the revelation of the founding mechanism." Girard, 233.

15. Including 1 Corinthians 12:3, Romans 10:9, and Philippians 2:11.

16. "The term *sacrament* finds its roots in the Roman empire's *sacramentum*, 'a sacred, public pledge of fidelity, symbolized by a visible sign such as a deposit of money or an oath of allegiance.' The imperial soldiers pledged the *sacramentum* as an oath of allegiance to their commander, the emperor and the gods of Rome. Tertullian and early Christian writers co-opted this symbol of imperial allegiance and described Christian baptism as a *sacramentum* that new recruits of the faith ritually professed, not to the emperor and his idols, but to their commander, the Christ. This baptismal *sacramentum* marked a new life of dedicated service to God in discipleship to the nonviolent Jesus. Baptism, like the *sacramentum*, sealed a permanent mark on the soul of the newborn Christian. It declared that this person belonged to Christ, not the emperor, and transformed the person into an instrument of God's love." John Dear, *The God of Peace: Toward A Theology of Nonviolence* (Eugene, Ore.: Wipf and Stock Publishers, 2005), 178.

17. "The king may have died, but the sacred quality of the sovereign still remains, and it remains a hungry god." Paul W. Kahn, *Sacred Violence: Torture, Terror, and Sovereignty* (Ann Arbor: University of Michigan Press, 2008), 34.

18. "Political meaning often enters the world through the killing and being killed of war. We take our first step towards torture when we take up arms in defense of the state. This is the step from law to sovereignty." Kahn, 14.

19. "The torturer acts as if he is at war, inflicting injury for the sake of a confession of defeat, but he does so within the borders of law. Kahn, 132.

20. Kahn, 100.

21. "The global rule of law and the global market were the most important projects of social construction at the beginning of the new millennium. The idea of a global order that transcends borders was only imaginable, however, to the extent that states felt no existential threat." Kahn, 142.

22. Kahn, 153.

23. Talal Asad, *On Suicide Bombing* (New York: Columbia University Press, 2007), 37-38.

24. At some points, Kahn acknowledges the fact that war can occur within a humanitarian framework, but he seems still to think of them as two different impulses in liberal societies rather than a part of a single mechanism. He says, "Even were warfare conducted within the rules of humanitarian law, that would no more eliminate

its underlying sacrificial quality than did the fact that torture in some European countries was subject to legal regulation." Kahn, *Sacred Violence*, 2008, 47. His point is that law is a concept foreign to sovereignty and overlaid on top of that existing logic, not that law necessarily perpetuates the sacrificial qualities of sovereignty.

25. Kahn, 142.

26. Kahn, 61.

27. "Just this asymmetry of dying without killing puts the fundamental tenant of Christianity beyond political experience in which being killed is always the license to kill." Kahn, 173.

28. Paul W. Kahn, *Sacred Violence: Torture, Terror, and Sovereignty* (Ann Arbor: University of Michigan Press, 2008), 34.

29. John D. Rempel, *The Lord's Supper in Anabaptism: A Study in the Christology of Balthasar Hubmaier, Pilgram Marpeck, and Dirk Philips* (Waterloo, Ont.; Scottdale, Pa.: Herald Press, 1993); Brian C. Brewer, *A Pledge of Love: Balthasar Hubmaier and Anabaptist Sacramentalism* (Milton Keynes, UK: Paternoster, 2014).

30. See previous discussion in Chapter 2, pp. 51-53.

31. Matthew 25:40.

Chapter Six

1. Martin Luther, "Lectures on Jonah," in *Luther's Works*, ed. Hilton Oswald, vol. 19 (St. Louis: Concordia Publishing House, 1974), 75-76.

2. Sallie McFague, *Models of God: Theology for an Ecological, Nuclear Age* (Philadelphia: Fortress Press, 1987).

3. John Bellamy Foster, *Marx's Ecology: Materialism and Nature* (New York: Monthly Review Press, 2000), 10-11.

4. Joerg Rieger, "Why Movements Matter Most: A Conversation with the New Materialism," in *Socialism in Process*, ed. Justin Heinzekehr and Philip Clayton (Process Century Press, 2017), 210.

5. Quoted in Stuart Elden, *Understanding Henri Lefebvre* (London: A&C Black, 2004), 35.

6. Rieger, "Why Movements Matter Most," 211.

7. Quoted in David Clough, "The Anxiety of the Human Animal: Martin Luther on Non-Human Animals and Human Animality," in *Creaturely Theology: On God, Humans and Other Animals*, ed. Celia Deane-Drummond and David Clough (London: SCM Press, 2009), 51.

8. Clough, 52.

9. Clough, 41.

10. Clough, 42.

11. Clough, 50.

12. This suggests that Foster is right in seeing anthropocentrism and romanticization as two sides of the same coin: "Yet, by focusing on the conflict between mechanism and vitalism or idealism (and losing sight of the more fundamental issue of materialism), one falls into a dualistic conception that fails to recognize that these

categories are dialectically connected in their one-sidedness, and must be tran-scended together." Foster, *Marx's Ecology*, 11.

13. Quoted in Philip M. Merklinger, *Philosophy, Theology, and Hegel's Berlin Philosophy of Religion, 1821-1827* (Albany, N.Y.: SUNY Press, 1993).

14. Quoted in Andrew Cole, "The Sacrament of the Fetish, the Miracle of the Commodity," in *The Legitimacy of the Middle Ages: On the Unwritten History of Theory*, ed. Andrew Cole and D. Vance Smith (Durham: Duke University Press Books, 2010), 78.

15. For example, Hegel dismisses the idea of an objective evolution of species along Darwinian lines: "A thinking consideration must reject such nebulous, at bottom, sensuous ideas, as in particular the so-called *origination*, for example, of plants and animals from water, and then the *origination* of the more highly developed animal organisms from the lower, and so on." Hegel regards this theory as inadequate precisely because "the utility of natural objects contains this truth, that they are not an absolute end in and for themselves. . . . The Notion [or Spirit] timelessly and in a universal manner posits all particularity in existence." Georg Wilhelm Friedrich Hegel, *Philosophy of Nature*, trans. A. V. Miller (Oxford: Clarendon Press, 2004), 20.

16. Karl Marx, *Capital: Volume 1*, trans. Ben Fowkes (London; New York: Penguin Classics, 1992), 163-65.

17. Cole, "The Sacrament of the Fetish, the Miracle of the Commodity," 78.

18. Cole, 77.

19. "It is in this 'misty realm of religion' that Marx takes something from Hegel's sacramental ideal in early Christianity—'Things heterogenous are here most intimately connected'—and calls it 'fetishism.' While Hegel would call those sacramental ideals 'feeling' and not 'fetishism,' he articulates fetishism as the reification of those very sacramental practices—any practice that translates feelings into Things for expropriative purposes." Cole, 79.

20. Foster, *Marx's Ecology*, 78.

21. An example would be Menno Simons' celestial flesh Christology, the idea that Jesus was not contaminated by Mary's flesh, since contact with the material world seemed to Menno to negate the divinity of Christ.

22. Heather Ann Ackley Bean, "Toward an Anabaptist/Mennonite Environmental Ethic," in *Creation and the Environment: An Anabaptist Perspective on a Sustainable World*, ed. Calvin Redekop (Baltimore; London: Johns Hopkins University Press, 2000), 186.

23. Karl Koop, "Migrations of Enchantment in the Radical Reformation: The Undoing of a Material and Natural World," in *Radicalizing Reformation: North American Perspectives*, ed. Karen L. Bloomquist, Craig L. Nessan, and Hans G. Ulrich (Zurich: LIT Verlag Münster, 2016), 259.

24. See Koop's suggestion that Radical Reformation traditions go back to Catholic or Orthodox views of incarnation. Koop, 262.

25. Karl Marx and Friedrich Engels, *The German Ideology* (International Publishers Co, 1972), 47.

26. Ched Myers, "From 'Creation Care' to 'Watershed Discipleship': Re-Placing Ecological Theology and Practice," *Conrad Grebel Review* 32, no. 3 (2014): 267.

27. Myers, 264.

Chapter Seven

1. James Cowan, *A Mapmaker's Dream: The Meditations of Fra Mauro, Cartographer to the Court of Venice* (Boston: Shambhala Publications, 2007), 101-104.

2. From John Snow's report, quoted in Edward Tufte, *Visual Explanations: Images and Quantities, Evidence and Narrative* (Cheshire, Conn.: Graphics Press, 1997), 27.

3. Tufte, 29.

4. Tufte, 32.

5. Tom Koch, "The Map as Intent: Variations on the Theme of John Snow," *Cartographica* 39, no. 4 (2004): 13.

6. For a summary of the Beck map and its significance, see Michael Bierut, "The Genius of the London Tube Map," March 2018, TED video, https://www.ted.com/talks/michael_bierut_the_genius_of_the_london_tube_map. For visual examples of the progression of subway map designs, see "The London Tube Map Archive," 24 May 2002, https://www.clarksbury.com/cdl/maps.html. Compare especially the difference between the 1908 and 1921 maps with Beck's 1933 version.

7. J. B. Harley, *The New Nature of Maps: Essays in the History of Cartography*, ed. Paul Laxton (Baltimore: Johns Hopkins University Press, 2001), 98.

8. Harley, 99.

9. "Maps such as those of John Smith . . . seem to show us an already tamed wilderness, one that has been rendered more acceptable to English eyes. . . . This sort of cartographic silence becomes an affirmative ideological act. It serves to prepare the way for European settlement. Potential settlers see, on the map, few obstacles that are insurmountable." Harley, 103-5.

10. Harley, 101.

11. Harley, 105.

12. Even a map like Borges describes in *A Universal History of Infamy*, which is so detailed that it covers the entire territory that it maps, could only show a single surface, and only one representation of the relations that constitute that surface. Peter Turchi, *Maps of the Imagination: The Writer as Cartographer* (San Antonio, Tex.: Trinity University Press, 2011), 37.

13. John D. Roth, *Choosing Against War: A Christian View* (Intercourse, Pa.: Good Books, 2002), 9.

14. John Winslade and Gerald D. Monk, *Narrative Mediation?: A New Approach to Conflict Resolution* (San Francisco: Jossey-Bass, 2000), 152.

15. "Because conflict tends to narrow people's focus onto things that support the ongoing life of the conflict, it is safe to assume that there will always be experience that lies outside the reach of the conflict story. These experiences will contradict, or at least not fit into, the conflict. . . . These outcomes are unique because they are often isolated pieces of lived experience that are not salient in people's thinking sim-

ply because they do not fit into the dominant story. In this sense they remain experiences subjugated beneath the weight of that story. We conceive of the mediator's task in this stage of the mediation process as listening for these unique outcomes or asking questions to elicit them and then seeking to build on them a counterstory to the conflict-saturated story." Winslade and Monk, 84.

16. William T. Cavanaugh, *The Myth of Religious Violence: Secular Ideology and the Roots of Modern Conflict* (Oxford University Press, 2009). See also Talal Asad, *On Suicide Bombing* (New York: Columbia University Press, 2007) for an analysis of the rhetoric of terrorism that justifies military action in the Middle East.

17. Reimer, *Mennonites and Classical Theology*.

18. John D. Caputo, *The Insistence of God: A Theology of Perhaps* (Bloomington, Ind.: Indiana University Press, 2013).

19. Peter Craig Blum, *For a Church to Come: Experiments in Postmodern Theory and Anabaptist Thought* (Harrisonburg, Va.: Herald Press, 2013), 153.

20. Rodriguez is a California-based artist who creates fictional maps or map-like images. Here cartography becomes a sort of visual language rather than a strictly geographical representation. See Rodriguez's portfolio at www.lordyrodriguez.com.

21. Michel Foucault, "What Is Enlightenment?," in *Ethics: Subjectivity and Truth*, ed. Paul Rabinow (New York: The New Press, 1997), 311.

22. I.e., John 12.

23. Matthew 28:8.

Conclusion

1. Jacques Derrida, *Specters of Marx: The State of the Debt, the Work of Mourning, and the New International* (New York: Routledge, 1994), 65.

2. Essentially, this idea of ecclesiological authority is parallel to Elisabeth Schussler Fiorenza's feminist hermeneutics: "A feminist critical interpretation of the Bible cannot take as its point of departure the normative authority of the biblical archetype, but must begin with women's experience in their struggle for liberation." Schüssler Fiorenza, *Bread Not Stone*, 13.

3. Ruth Krall, *The Elephant in God's Living Room*, vol. 1 (n.p., 2012), x, https://ruthkrall.com/downloadable-books/elephants-in-gods-living-room-volume-one/.

BIBLIOGRAPHY

Alliez, Eric. *The Signature of the World, or, What Is Deleuze and Guattari's Philosophy?* London; New York: Continuum, 2004.

Asad, Talal. *On Suicide Bombing.* New York: Columbia University Press, 2007.

Baird, Marie L. "Revisioning Christian Theology in Light of Emmanuel Levinas's Ethics of Responsibility." *Journal of Ecumenical Studies* 36, no. 3–4 (1999): 340-351.

Barth, Karl. *Church Dogmatics.* Vol. 1.2. Edinburgh: T. & T. Clark, 1936.

Bean, Heather Ann Ackley. "Toward an Anabaptist/Mennonite Environmental Ethic." In *Creation and the Environment: An Anabaptist Perspective on a Sustainable World,* ed. Calvin Redekop, 183-205. Baltimore; London: Johns Hopkins University Press, 2000.

Blum, Peter Craig. *For a Church to Come: Experiments in Postmodern Theory and Anabaptist Thought.* Harrisonburg, Va.: Herald Press, 2013.

Brady, Thomas A., Jr. "'You Hate Us Priests': Anticlericalism, Communalism, and the Control of Women at Strasbourg in the Age of the Reformation." In *Anticlericalism in Late Medieval and Early Modern Europe,* ed. Peter A. Dykema and Heiko Augustinus Oberman, 167-207. Leiden: Brill, 1993.

Braght, Thieleman J. van. *The Bloody Theater, or, Martyrs Mirror.* Trans. Joseph F. Sohm. 5th ed. Scottdale, Pa.: Herald Press, 1950.

Brewer, Brian C. *A Pledge of Love: Balthasar Hubmaier and Anabaptist Sacramentalism.* Milton Keynes, UK: Paternoster, 2014.

Caputo, John D. *The Insistence of God: A Theology of Perhaps.* Bloomington, Ind.: Indiana University Press, 2013.

Cavanaugh, William T. *The Myth of Religious Violence: Secular Ideology and the Roots of Modern Conflict.* New York: Oxford University Press, 2009.

———. *The Myth of Religious Violence: Secular Ideology and the Roots of Modern Conflict.* Oxford University Press, 2009.

Clough, David. "The Anxiety of the Human Animal: Martin Luther on Non-Human Animals and Human Animality." In *Creaturely Theology: On God, Humans and Other Animals*, ed. Celia Deane-Drummond and David Clough, 41-60. London: SCM Press, 2009.

Coakley, Sarah. *Powers and Submissions: Spirituality, Philosophy, and Gender*. Oxford; Malden, Mass.: Blackwell Publishers, 2002.

Cobb, John B., and David Ray Griffin. *Process Theology: An Introductory Exposition*. Philadelphia: Westminster Press, 1976.

Cole, Andrew. "The Sacrament of the Fetish, the Miracle of the Commodity." In *The Legitimacy of the Middle Ages: On the Unwritten History of Theory*, ed. Andrew Cole and D. Vance Smith, 70-93. Durham: Duke University Press Books, 2010.

Colombo, Joseph A. "God as Hidden, God as Manifest: 'Who Is the Subject of Salvation in History in Liberation Theology?'" *The Journal of Religion* 71, no. 1 (1991): 18-35.

Cone, James H. *A Black Theology of Liberation*. 20th anniversary ed. Maryknoll, N.Y.: Orbis Books, 1990.

Cowan, James. *A Mapmaker's Dream: The Meditations of Fra Mauro, Cartographer to the Court of Venice*. Boston: Shambhala Publications, 2007.

Cramer, David. "Mennonite Systematic Theology in Retrospect and Prospect." *Conrad Grebel Review* 31, no. 3 (Fall 2013): 255-273.

Dear, John. *The God of Peace: Toward A Theology of Nonviolence*. Eugene, Ore.: Wipf and Stock Publishers, 2005.

Deleuze, Gilles. *Difference and Repetition*. Trans. Paul Patton. Revised ed. New York: Columbia University Press, 1995.

Deleuze, Gilles, and Félix Guattari. *A Thousand Plateaus: Capitalism and Schizophrenia*. London: Continuum, 2004.

Derrida, Jacques. *Specters of Marx: The State of the Debt, the Work of Mourning, and the New International*. New York: Routledge, 1994.

Dykema, Peter A., and Heiko Augustinus Oberman, eds. *Anticlericalism in Late Medieval and Early Modern Europe*. Leiden: Brill, 1993.

Ehrman, Bart D. *Jesus: Apocalyptic Prophet of the New Millennium*. Oxford: Oxford University Press, 1999.

Elden, Stuart. *Understanding Henri Lefebvre*. London: A&C Black, 2004.

Enns, Elaine. "Pilgrimage to the Ukraine: Revisioning History through Restorative Justice." Bartimaeus Cooperative Ministries. Accessed January 10, 2015. http://www.bcm-net.org/pilgrimage-to-the-ukraine-revisioning-history-through-restorative-justice-elaine-enns.

Euler, Carrie. "Huldrych Zwingli and Heinrich Bullinger." In *A Companion to the Eucharist in the Reformation*, ed. Lee Palmer Wandel, 57-74. Leiden: Brill, 2014.

Finger, Thomas N. "Appropriating Other Traditions While Remaining Anabaptist." *Conrad Grebel Review* 17, no. 2 (1999): 52-68.

Ford, Lewis S. *Transforming Process Theism*. Albany, N.Y.: State University of New York Press, 2000.

Foster, John Bellamy. *Marx's Ecology: Materialism and Nature*. New York: Monthly Review Press, 2000.

Foucault, Michel. "What Is Enlightenment?" In *Ethics: Subjectivity and Truth*, ed. Paul Rabinow, 303-319. New York: The New Press, 1997.

Frascati-Lochhead, Marta. *Kenosis and Feminist Theology: The Challenge of Gianni Vattimo*. Albany, N.Y.: State University of New York Press, 1998.

Friedman, Richard Elliott. *The Hidden Face of God*. Harper Collins, 1996.

Gillespie, Michael Allen. *The Theological Origins of Modernity*. Chicago: University Of Chicago Press, 2009.

Girard, Rene. *Things Hidden Since the Foundation of the World*. Trans. Stephen Bann and Michael Metter. Stanford, Calif.: Stanford University Press, 1987.

Goertz, Hans-Jürgen. "Karlstadt, Muntzer and the Reformation of the Commoners, 1521-1525." In *A Companion to Anabaptism and Spiritualism, 1521-1700*, ed. John Roth and James Stayer, 1-44. Leiden: Brill, 2007.

———. *The Anabaptists*. Trans. Trevor Johnson. London: Routledge, 1996.

Goossen, Rachel Waltner. "'Defanging the Beast': Mennonite Responses to John Howard Yoder's Sexual Abuse." *Mennonite Quarterly Review* 89, no. 1 (2015): 7-80.

Gregory of Nyssa. *The Life of Moses*. Mahwah, N.J.: Paulist Press, 1978.

Hardie, Philip. *Ovid's Poetics of Illusion*. Cambridge; New York: Cambridge University Press, 2002.

Harley, J. B. *The New Nature of Maps: Essays in the History of Cartography*. Ed. Paul Laxton. Baltimore: Johns Hopkins University Press, 2001.

Heath, Jane M.F. "Absent Presences of Paul and Christ: Enargeia in 1 Thessalonians 1-3." *Journal for the Study of the New Testament* 32, no. 1 (2009): 3-38.

Hegel, Georg Wilhelm Friedrich. *Philosophy of Nature*. Trans. A. V. Miller. Oxford: Clarendon Press, 2004.

Heinzekehr, Justin. "A Critique of Pure Justice: The Antinomy of John Howard Yoder." *Mennonite Life* 68, no. 1 (2014). http://archive.bethelks.edu/ml/issue/vol-68/article/a-critique-of-pure-justice-the-antinomy-of-john-ho/.

Hubmaier, Balthasar. "On the Christian Ban." In *Balthasar Hubmaier, Theologian of Anabaptism*, trans. H. Wayne Pipkin and John Howard Yoder, 409-425. Scottdale, Pa.: Herald Press, 1989.

———. "Several Theses Concerning the Mass." In *Balthasar Hubmaier, Theologian of Anabaptism*, trans. H. Wayne Pipkin and John Howard Yoder, 73-77. Scottdale, Pa.: Herald Press, 1989.

Iggers, Georg G. *Historiography in the Twentieth Century: From Scientific Objectivity to the Postmodern Challenge*. Middletown, Conn.: Wesleyan University Press, 2005.

Isasi-Díaz, Ada María. *En La Lucha (In the Struggle): A Hispanic Women's Liberation Theology*. Minneapolis: Fortress Press, 1993.

Jensen, Robin Margaret. *Understanding Early Christian Art*. London; New York: Routledge, 2013.

Julian of Norwich. *Revelations of Divine Love*. Trans. Frances Beer. Cambridge: D.S. Brewer, 1998.

Kahn, Paul W. *Sacred Violence: Torture, Terror, and Sovereignty*. Ann Arbor: University of Michigan Press, 2008.

———. *Sacred Violence: Torture, Terror, and Sovereignty*. Ann Arbor: University of Michigan Press, 2008.

Kant, Immanuel. *Critique of Judgement*. Ed. Nicholas Walker. Trans. James Creed Meredith. Oxford: Oxford University Press, 2009.

Keller, Catherine. *Face of the Deep: A Theology of Becoming*. London: Routledge, 2003.

———. "The Mystery of the Insoluble Evil: Violence and Evil in Marjorie Suchocki." In *World Without End: Christian Eschatology from a Process Perspective*, ed. Joseph A. Bracken, 46-71. Grand Rapids, Mich.: Eerdmans, 2005.

Kennel, Maxwell. "Mennonite Metaphysics? Exploring the Philosophical Aspects of Mennonite Theology from Pacifist Epistemology to Ontological Peace." *Mennonite Quarterly Review* 91, no. 3 (2017): 403-421.

Koch, Tom. "The Map as Intent: Variations on the Theme of John Snow." *Cartographica* 39, no. 4 (2004): 1-14.

Koop, Karl. "Migrations of Enchantment in the Radical Reformation: The Undoing of a Material and Natural World." In *Radicalizing Reformation: North American Perspectives*, ed. Karen L. Bloomquist, Craig L. Nessan, and Hans G. Ulrich, 243-264. Zurich: LIT Verlag Münster, 2016.

Krall, Ruth. *The Elephant in God's Living Room*. Vol. 1. n.p., 2012. https://ruthkrall.com/downloadable-books/elephants-in-gods-living-room-volume-one/.

———. *The Elephant in God's Living Room*. Vol. 3. n.p., 2013. https://ruthkrall.com/downloadable-books/volume-three-the-mennonite-church-and-john-howard-yoder-collected-essays/.

Krehbiel, Stephanie. "Staying Alive: How Martyrdom Made Me a Warrior." *Mennonite Life* 61, no. 4 (2006). http://archive.bethelks.edu/ml/issue/vol-61-no-4/.

Lamm, Julia A. "A Guide to Christian Mysticism." In *The Wiley-Blackwell Companion to Christian Mysticism*, 1-24. Hoboken, N.J.: John Wiley & Sons, 2017.

Lee, Eojin. *Theology of the Open Table*. Eugene, Ore.: Wipf and Stock Publishers, 2016.

Lévinas, Emmanuel. *Emmanuel Levinas: Basic Philosophical Writings*. Bloomington, Ind.: Indiana University Press, 1996.

———. *Totality and Infinity: An Essay on Exteriority*. Trans. Alphonso Lingis. The Hague: M. Nijhoff Publishers, 1979.

Lind, Millard. *Yahweh Is a Warrior: The Theology of Warfare in Ancient Israel.* Scottdale, Pa.: Herald Press, 1980.

Luther, Martin. "Lectures on Jonah." In *Luther's Works*, ed. Hilton Oswald, 19:3-104. St. Louis: Concordia Publishing House, 1974.

Lyotard, Jean-François. *The Differend: Phrases in Dispute.* Minneapolis: University of Minnesota Press, 1988.

MacGregor, Kirk R. *A Central European Synthesis of Radical and Magisterial Reform: The Sacremental Theology of Balthasar Hubmaier.* Lanham, Md.: University Press of America, 2006.

———. "The Eucharistic Theology and Ethics of Balthasar Hubmaier." *Harvard Theological Review* 105, no. 2 (2012): 223-445.

Magnússon, Sigurður Gylfi, and István M. Szijártó, eds. *What Is Microhistory?* Routledge, 2013.

Marin, Juan. "A Lukan Kenosis? Luke's Concept of Truth as an Ethics of Service." *Journal of Philosophy and Scripture* 6, no. 1 (2009): 1-8.

Marpeck, Pilgram. *The Writings of Pilgram Marpeck.* Ed. William Klassen and Walter Klaassen. Kitchener, Ont.; Scottdale, Pa.: Herald Press, 1978.

Marx, Karl. *Capital: Volume 1.* Trans. Ben Fowkes. London; New York: Penguin Classics, 1992.

———. *Capital: Volume 3.* Trans. David Fernbach. London; New York: Penguin Classics, 1992.

Marx, Karl, and Friedrich Engels. *The German Ideology.* International Publishers Co, 1972.

Mast, Gerald. "Pacifism as a Way of Knowing." In *John Howard Yoder: Radical Theologian*, ed. J. Denny Weaver, 226-243. Eugene, Ore.: Cascade Books, 2014.

———. "Sin and Failure in Anabaptist Theology." In *John Howard Yoder: Radical Theologian*, ed. J. Denny Weaver, 351-370. Eugene, Ore.: Cascade Books, 2014.

McFague, Sallie. *Models of God: Theology for an Ecological, Nuclear Age.* Philadelphia: Fortress Press, 1987.

McGrath, Alister E. *Luther's Theology of the Cross: Martin Luther's Theological Breakthrough.* Oxford: Blackwell, 1985.

Merklinger, Philip M. *Philosophy, Theology, and Hegel's Berlin Philosophy of Religion, 1821-1827.* Albany, N.Y.: SUNY Press, 1993.

Myers, Ched. "From 'Creation Care' to 'Watershed Discipleship': Re-Placing Ecological Theology and Practice." *Conrad Grebel Review* 32, no. 3 (2014): 150-175.

Nixon, Gregory. "Whitehead and the Elusive Present: Process Philosophy's Creative Core." *Journal of Consciousness Exploration & Research* 1, no. 5 (2010): 625-639.

Packull, Werner O. *Hutterite Beginnings: Communitarian Experiments during the Reformation.* Baltimore, Md: Johns Hopkins University Press, 1995.

Partee, Charles. *Calvin and Classical Philosophy*. Louisville, Ky.: Westminster John Knox Press, 2005.

Plett, Heinrich F. *Enargeia in Classical Antiquity and the Early Modern Age: The Aesthetics of Evidence*. Leiden: Brill, 2012.

Reimer, A. James. *Mennonites and Classical Theology: Dogmatic Foundations for Christian Ethics*. Kitchener, Ont.: Pandora Press, 2001.

Rempel, John D. *The Lord's Supper in Anabaptism: A Study in the Christology of Balthasar Hubmaier, Pilgram Marpeck, and Dirk Philips*. Waterloo, Ont.; Scottdale, Pa.: Herald Press, 1993.

Rieger, Joerg. "Why Movements Matter Most: A Conversation with the New Materialism." In *Socialism in Process*, ed. Justin Heinzekehr and Philip Clayton, 205-228. Process Century Press, 2017.

Robinette, Brian DuWayne. *Grammars of Resurrection: A Christian Theology of Presence and Absence*. New York: Crossroad Pub. Co, 2009.

Roth, John D. *Choosing Against War: A Christian View*. Intercourse, Pa.: Good Books, 2002.

Rothkegel, Martin. "Pilgram Marpeck and the Fellows of the Covenant: The Short and Fragmentary History of the Rise and Decline of an Anabaptist Denominational Network." *Mennonite Quarterly Review* 85, no. 1 (2011): 7-36.

Ruether, Rosemary Radford. *Sexism and God-Talk: Toward a Feminist Theology*. Boston: Beacon Press, 1983.

Schüssler Fiorenza, Elisabeth. *Bread Not Stone: The Challenge of Feminist Biblical Interpretation*. Beacon Press, 1995.

———. *Jesus: Miriam's Child, Sophia's Prophet*. New York: Continuum, 1995.

Smith, Daniel Alan. *Revisiting the Empty Tomb: The Early History of Easter*. Minneapolis: Fortress Press, 2010.

Smith, Wilfred Cantwell. *The Meaning and End of Religion*. Minneapolis: Fortress Press, 1964.

Sobrino, Jon. *Jesus the Liberator: A Historical-Theological Reading of Jesus of Nazareth*. Trans. Paul Burns and Francis McDonagh. Maryknoll, N.Y.: Orbis Books, 1993.

Sorensen, Rob. *Martin Luther and the German Reformation*. London: Anthem, 2016.

Stayer, James. "Introduction." In *A Companion to Anabaptism and Spiritualism, 1521-1700*, xxiii-xxiv. Leiden: Brill, 2007.

Suchocki, Marjorie. *The End of Evil: Process Eschatology in Historical Context*. Albany, N.Y.: State University of New York Press, 1988.

Tufte, Edward. *Visual Explanations: Images and Quantities, Evidence and Narrative*. Cheshire, Conn.: Graphics Press, 1997.

Turchi, Peter. *Maps of the Imagination: The Writer as Cartographer*. San Antonio, Tex.: Trinity University Press, 2011.

Vegetius. *Epitome of Military Science*. Trans. N. P. Milner. Liverpool: Liverpool University Press, 1996.

Weaver, J. Denny. *The Nonviolent God*. Grand Rapids, Mich.: Eerdmans, 2013.

Webb, Ruth. *Ekphrasis, Imagination and Persuasion in Ancient Rhetorical Rheory and Practice*. Farnham, Surrey; Burlington, Vt.: Ashgate, 2009.

Whitehead, Alfred North. *Process and Reality*. Corrected ed. New York: Free Press, 1978.

Widder, Nathan. *Political Theory after Deleuze*. London: Continuum International Pub. Group, 2015.

Winslade, John, and Gerald D. Monk. *Narrative Mediation?: A New Approach to Conflict Resolution*. San Francisco: Jossey-Bass, 2000.

Yoder, John Howard. *For the Nations: Essays Evangelical and Public*. Grand Rapids, Mich.: Eerdmans, 1997.

———. *He Came Preaching Peace*. Scottdale, Pa.: Herald Press, 1985.

———. *Preface to Theology: Christology and Theological Method*. Grand Rapids, Mich.: Brazos Press, 2002.

———, ed. *The Schleitheim Confession*. Scottdale, Pa.: Herald Press, 1977.

THE INDEX

A

Abraham (Patriarch), 90-91
Akhnai, oven of, 18-21, 33
Anabaptism, 31, 60, 74, 79-83, 113-118, 134n27
Ecclesiology, 51-53
Sacramental theology, 25-26, 94, 103-106
Sixteenth century, 46, 51-57, 70-71, 104, 125, 132n9, 133n18, 134n30, 138n13
Anabaptist Vision, 140n42
Anticlericalism, 25, 47-48, 50, 126, 131n6, 132n7-8
Anti-foundationalism, 54, 71, 81, 134n27, 138n14
Anthropocentrism, 26, 96-100, 104, 121, 142n12
Aquinas, Thomas, 48, 53
Asad, Talal, 91

B

Barth, Karl, 86, 140n3
Bean, Heather, 104
Beck, Harry, 111, 113-114, 144n6
Bible
    Acts (Book), 18, 22-23
    Colossians (Book), 72
    1 Corinthians, 38-39
    Exodus (Book), 62
    Gospels, 18, 22, 31-32, 72, 80, 85-89, 92, 124, 140n40, 141n14
    Empty tomb narrative, 24-25, 31-44, 45, 57, 113
    Isaiah (Book), 32-33
    Leviticus, 19
    Luke (Book), 38, 40, 42-43
    Mark (Book), 38-39, 130n20
    Matthew (Book), 23, 38, 43, 82, 88, 94, 124
    Psalms, 32, 97, 129n3
    Philippians (Book), 39-40, 129n13
    1 Thessalonians, 42
Bioregionalism, 105-106
Blum, Peter, 117
Bonino, José Míguez, 68

C

Calvin, John, 25, 50-53, 133n15
Capitalism, 67, 102, 136n13
Cavanaugh, William, 116
Coakley, Sarah, 39-40, 129n13

153

Cobb, John, 77
Cole, Andrew, 102
Colonialism, 67, 71, 111-112, 117, 137n5
Cosmology, 17, 25, 72-73
Consensus, 20-23, 27, 54-55, 82, 121-123, 128n6
Constantine, 80
Cowan, James, 107
Cramer, David, 134n27

D
Deep ecology, 98
Deleuze, Gilles, 62, 67-68
Derrida, Jacques, 71, 121
Deus absconditus, 46, 48-49
Deuteronomy, 20, 33
Dialectic, 18, 20, 99-103, 143n12
Dionysius of Halicarnassus, 41
Domestication, 25, 44, 61-62, 65-66, 122
Donkov, Jivko, 135n33

E
Ecclesiology, 51, 74, 94, 104, 117, 124-126, 145n2
Ecology/environment, 26, 71, 74, 96-106, 107, 120-121, 127
Enargeia, 25, 41-44, 59, 64
Enns, Elaine, 71, 137n5
Epistemology, 53-55, 68
Erasmus, 49
Eschatology, 71, 73, 82, 138n14
Eucharist, 48-55, 93, 100-104, 121, 125, 133n15, 134n22

F
Finger, Thomas, 138n14
Ford, Lewis, 77-79
Foster, John Bellamy, 98, 142n12
Foucault, Michel, 67, 71, 118

Foundationalism, 54, 71, 81, 134n27, 138n14
Friedman, Richard, 33

G
Genesis, 40, 97, 100
Gibson, Mel, 116
Gillespie, Michael, 131n4
Girard, Rene, 25-26, 85-89, 92, 94
Goertz, Hans-Ju?rgen, 131n7
Google, 112
Goossen, Rachel Waltner, 14
Gregory of Nyssa, 45, 130n21

H
Harley, J.B., 111
Heath, Jane, 42
Hegel, G. W. F., 26, 99-105, 143n15, 143n19
Hermeneutics, 20, 54, 80-81, 130n19, 145n2
Hubmaier, Balthasar, 25, 45, 51-55, 60, 93-94, 103-105, 125, 133n17-22

I
Immanence, 73, 76, 80, 94
Incarnation, 39-40, 78-79, 97, 106, 130n19

J
John (Book), 22, 38, 72
John of the Cross, 45
Julian of Norwich, 45
Justin Martyr, 40

K
Kahn, Paul, 25-26, 55, 85-86, 89-92, 141n24
Kant, Immanuel, 63-64
Karlstadt, Andreas, 50

Keller, Catherine, 25, 77-79, 140n40
Kennel, Maxwell, 137n3
Kenosis, 25, 39-41
Koop, Karl, 104, 144n24
Krall, Ruth, 14, 126

L

Law, 22-23, 67, 85, 89-92, 121, 141n18-21, 142n24
Lefebvre, Henri, 99
Levinas, Emmanuel, 25, 43, 55, 58, 65, 106, 122, 131n31, 136n12, 145n2
Liberation theology, 23-26, 39, 68, 122-126, 129n6, 130n19, 135n4
Lind, Millard, 137n6
Lucretius, 42
Luther, Martin, 25, 48-53, 70, 96, 99-106, 118, 133n15
Lyotard, Jean-François, 82, 137n4

M

MacGregor, Kirk, 52, 133n17, 134n22
Marginalization, 18, 23-24, 31, 53, 59, 81, 93-94, 106, 113, 123, 125
Marin, Juan, 40
Marpeck, Pilgram, 54
Marx, Karl, 26, 67, 99-105, 125, 136n13, 143n19
Mast, Gerald, 129n13
Materialism, 17-18, 25-26, 52-54, 60, 96-105, 120, 143n12
McFague, Sallie, 97
McGrath, Alister, 49, 132n11
Mennonites, 55-56, 71, 114, 117, 137n3, 137n5, 140n42
Theology, 79, 105, 125-126,
134n27, 138n13, 139n36
Metaphysics, 17-18, 96, 107, 121, 126, 137n2-3, 138n7
Kenotic, 40, 130n14, 130n19
Process metaphysics, 24-25, 69, 70-83, 113, 138n12
Sacramental, 48, 101-104
Microhistory, 72-73, 80, 138n8, 138n11
Micrometaphysics, 72, 80, 138n12
Monk, Gerald, 115
Myers, Ched, 105-106
Mysticism, 23-24, 45-46, 131n3

N

Narrative, 24-26, 56, 71-72, 115-116, 122, 137n4
Empty tomb, 32-33, 38-43, 59, 71-72
New Materialism, 98-99
Nominalism, 46-49, 53, 70, 131n4, 134n26, 137n2
Nonviolence, 24, 65, 71, 79, 88, 94, 107, 137n6, 141n16
As creative, 26, 81, 114-119
Epistemological, 54-55

O

Omnipresence, 27, 69, 133n21
Ontology, 51-52, 76, 103, 122, 133n18, 138n7
Other, 73, 112, 135n5
As transcendent, 25, 55-56, 58-68, 94, 121-122, 131n31, 135n7, 136n11

P

Pacifism, 14, 94, 107-108, 114-119, 137n6
Paul (Apostle), 38-40, 42, 45, 88, 130n15

Pentecost, 22, 41
Plato, 75, 77
Pneumatology, 78-79
Political theology, 24-25, 53-57, 85-
   95, 121
Power, 39-41, 47-48, 50, 53, 56, 78,
   111-114, 122
   In communities, 14, 21-25, 82-
   83, 124, 140n42
   Relation to sacred, 17, 21-25,
   59-68, 106-107, 136n7
Process theology, 25, 69, 70-81

R
Race, 61, 64-68, 117-118, 136n12
Radical Reformation, 25, 44, 48-57,
   104, 143n24
Rahner, Karl, 132n10
Reformation, 24, 45-58, 66, 84, 93,
   99-100, 131n6, 132n8
   Radical, 25, 44, 48-57, 104,
   143n24
Reimer, James, 79-82, 117, 138n13-
   14
Rempel, John, 133n17, 134n22
Rhetoric, 25, 41-42, 47, 57, 145n16
Rieger, Joerg, 98-99
Rodriguez, Lordy, 118, 145n20
Romanticization, 26, 96-106, 121,
   142n12
Roth, John, 114-115
Ruether, Rosemary Radford, 130n14

S
Sacrament, 17-18, 84-85, 89, 99-
   106, 121, 141n16, 143n19
   Reformation theology, 25-26,
   48-57, 93-94, 99-100, 113,
   117, 133n18-22
Sacredness, 23, 59, 64-67, 97, 122-
   123

Empty tomb, 59, 113,
Sacraments, 17, 25, 49, 53-54, 99-
   106, 141n16
Sovereignty, 26, 84-90, 92, 140n9,
   141n17
Sacrifice, 26, 55-56, 59-60, 84-94,
   103, 140n7, 140n9, 141n14,
   142n24
Salvation, 25, 47, 49, 53, 82
Scholasticism, 46, 48-49, 70, 137n2
Schüssler Fiorenza, Elizabeth, 39,
   145n2
Secularism, 44, 58-59, 70, 85, 103,
   116, 123-125, 130n19
Self, 25-26, 52-55, 60-69, 73, 83,
   96, 108, 113-114, 121-122
Simons, Menno, 143n21
Smith, Daniel, 38
Snow, John, 108-110, 113-114
Sovereignty, 26, 55-57, 84-95, 96,
   121, 135n3, 141n17-18,
   142n24
   Other, 62, 92-95, 135n7
Stayer, James, 132n9
Sublime, 62-64, 136n10

T
Talmud, 18-23
Tertullian, 141n16
Topography, 26, 61-62, 67, 69, 83,
   111, 113, 117, 124
Transcendence, 48, 73-78, 81-82,
   89-91, 132n10, 141n14
   Christ, 18, 24, 39, 85, 91, 117
   Other, 59-62, 106, 131n31,
   136n7
Trump, Donald, 64
Tufte, Edward, 109

U
Universality, 71-73, 85, 91-92, 121

V
Vegetius, 84

W
Weaver, J. Denny, 137n6
Whitehead, Alfred North, 25, 70,
    73-78, 83, 113, 138n12,
    139n15
Willems, Dirk, 55-57, 58-60,
    135n33
William of Ockham, 46-47, 131n4
Winslade, John, 115

Y
Yoder, John Howard, 14, 74, 81-82,
    128n6, 129n13, 130n15,
    134n27, 140n40, 140n42

Z
Zwingli, Ulrich, 25, 50-53, 103,
    133n15, 133n18

THE AUTHOR

Justin Heinzekehr is Director of Institutional Research and Assessment and Assistant Professor of Bible and Religion at Goshen College. His most recent work has focused on the intersection of political philosophy, religion, and environmental ethics, with titles such as *Organic Marxism* (2014) and *Socialism in Process* (2017).

CPSIA information can be obtained
at www.ICGtesting.com
Printed in the USA
FSHW022319301119
64446FS

9 781680 270143